Getting
HEALED

a guide to receive healing

Derek Walker

DESTINY IMAGE™ EUROPE srl
Via Maiella, I
66020 San Giovanni Teatino (Ch) – Italy

"Changing the world, one book at a time."

This book and all other Destiny Image™ Europe books are available at Christian bookstores and distributors worldwide.

To order products, or for any other correspondence:

DESTINY IMAGE™ EUROPE srl
Via della Scafa 29/14
65013 Città Sant'Angelo (Pe), Italy
Tel. +39 085 4716623 • +39 085 8670146
Email: info@eurodestinyimage.com
Or reach us on the Internet: www.eurodestinyimage.com

ISBN 13: 978-88-96727-34-8
ISBN 13 Ebook: 978-88-96727-38-6

For Worldwide Distribution, Printed in Italy
I 2 3 4 5 6/14 I3 I2 II

Dedication

I dedicate this book to my lovely and gifted wife, Hilary, who has been such a wonderful and faithful helpmeet. It was her dramatic healing from arthritis, described in this book, that played a part in the Lord bringing us together. Without her love and sacrifices for me, I could not do what I do, and I want to thank her from the bottom of my heart, especially in supporting my writing of this book, which has consumed much of my spare time.

Acknowledgments

I also want to acknowledge a number of excellent Bible teachers who have helped in the development of my understanding of divine healing from the Scriptures, including Roger Price, Derek Prince, Kenneth Hagin, Doug Jones, Keith Moore, and Bob Yandian.

Endorsements

Derek and Hilary Walker attended my church and were enrolled in our ministerial school. It was obvious from the beginning that Derek had a call on his life to rightly divide and teach the Word of God. He has more than proved this at the church he pastors, Oxford Bible Church. His book, *Getting Healed*, has blessed me and taught me areas of healing I did not know. You too will learn about God's gift of healing and how you can be guided into God's healing power. Please read it and pass it on to others.

Reverend Bob Yandian
Pastor, Grace Church
Tulsa, Oklahoma

The subject of healing continues to be surrounded with skepticism, but Pastor Derek Walker has given the world a healing manual persuasively written with unusual clarity. As a healing evangelist, I recognize the spirit of faith when I see it, and this book is remarkably faith-filled, sustaining the spirit of faith page after page, and assuring us indisputably that healing is a benefit included in the atonement. You cannot help but be healed when you encounter the truth in these pages!

Christine Darg
Evangelist and International Preacher

Pastor Derek Walker is one of the greatest Christian teachers and writers we have today. His materials are well-researched in order to keep you well-informed about the subject matter. This book about how to receive your healing is long overdue. It is loaded with information that will help you as a Christian to go directly to your heavenly Father to receive the free gift of healing He has for you, rather than chasing men all over the place and wasting valuable time. It contains practical information to help align you with the will and the Word of God in order to access the gift of healing from God. I hope and pray you will have a life-transforming encounter with the Lord as you go through the pages of this book.

Yemi Balogun
Revelation TV presentor

This is the perfect book to place in someone's hands if they are struggling to receive healing. Derek has not only written it, he lives it and practices it now—and you can too! You'll be in no doubt: Jesus still heals today!

Gordon Hickson

Jesus said, "Therefore I say unto you,
whatsoever things you desire,
when you pray,
believe that you receive them,
and you will have them"
(Mark 11:24 KJV).

Contents

Foreword

I have had the privilege of knowing Derek Walker and his wife, Hilary, for nearly 20 years at the time of the release of his book on healing. Denise and I have had the privilege of ministering in his church in Oxford, England.

During those years I have found him to be a minister who studies with great depth. Yet, when he teaches, he always has the heart and compassion of a pastor—breaking apart the Word of God so that even the youngest Christian can grasp its meaning. So whether he is discussing end times or the new birth, you can be sure that Derek has done his homework. Still he communicates with a humility and gentle spirit that is refreshing. His goal is simply to edify, encourage, and instruct those whom he is teaching.

In this volume on the subject of healing, Derek has done it again. *Getting Healed* demonstrates the precision of a mathematically trained Oxford graduate, the vitality of a graduate of a Spirit-filled Bible college, and the heart of a pastor encouraging his sheep. Derek truly brings his academic training and pastoral experience to the subject of healing.

And from the very opening of this book, he makes his most critical point: healing comes from the Lord. While he goes on to outline an outstanding series of practical steps for individuals to take to receive healing, he avoids the error of so many on this subject—making it sound as if by these mere steps we heal ourselves. The graciousness of God and His place as Healer are properly placed as the foundation of all biblical healing. And upon this foundation, he then lays out the practical, personal steps that each person should take. Grace and response, the very heart of the Bible brought to this vital subject of physical healing.

Everyone studying the subject of healing will find this volume profitable and practical. It is my honor to commend this volume to you.

Rick Renner*, Senior Pastor
Moscow Good News Church

*Rick Renner is a highly respected Christian leader. He is the author of more than 20 books as well as a Bible teacher. He has also founded the Riga and Kiev Good News Churches and is the founder and director of the Good News Association consisting of about 800 churches. His Christian television network broadcasts the Gospel across the entire former USSR.

Introduction

YOU CAN RECEIVE HEALING!

Our health is one of the most important things we possess. We all want and need to be in good health. We know that being healthy is vital for us in order to enjoy life, as well as to fulfill God's will for our lives.

Yet because sickness is so common, we accept it as if it were normal. There is much uncertainty among Christians about whether healing is God's will, or how we can be healed. Hopes are raised by hearing wonderful testimonies of healing, but equally we are aware of those who don't get healed.

Many conclude that healing is a hit or miss affair; that sometimes God wants to heal us, but often in His sovereignty He chooses otherwise. As a result, when it comes to receiving healing for ourselves, we lack confidence, feeling that we are on shaky ground. We pray, but when nothing seems to change we can easily resign ourselves to the sickness, perhaps even submitting to it as God's will for us. To help us feel better, we construct explanations as to why God does not want to heal us yet. Perhaps He is trying to teach us something, or perfect our character.

If we try to understand God's will from what our eyes see in the world around us or from our experiences and feelings, we will remain in confusion. So much of what happens in this fallen world is clearly *not* God's will, so that cannot be used to judge His will. God's will is certainly done in Heaven, but not necessarily on earth, for Jesus told us to pray, "...Your will be done on earth as it is in Heaven" (Matt. 6:10). Now there is surely no sickness in Heaven! That should be a sign to us that healing is God's will. Through believing prayer (based on God's will in Heaven), we can also bring God's will (healing) to pass in the earth. In fact, every time and place where we see God's perfect will, there is no sickness, such as in the Garden of Eden before the Fall, or in the future eternal Kingdom of God.

Sickness and death came into the world as part of the curse of sin. It was man's sin that opened the door to sickness. Sickness is our enemy. How dare we say it is God's will for His children!

This book is written to clear away all the confusion around this subject by bringing you back to the simplicity of God's Word concerning your healing. It is designed to systematically build your faith and confidence in God's promises until you are fully persuaded that healing belongs to you as a New Covenant child of God. Then you will find yourself well able to come to your loving and generous heavenly Father and freely receive your healing.

I want you to know that whatever sickness you are facing there is *hope* for you to be healed. God says to you, "I know the thoughts [plans] that I think toward you," says the Lord, "thoughts of peace [wholeness, healing] and not of evil, to give you a future and a hope" (Jer. 29:11). Evil here is set in contrast to peace (shalom, health), and so it includes sickness. God loves you passionately and He wants to heal you more than you could possibly know. He has abundant healing for you, but you need to learn how to receive it.

I want you to cast away the idea that God does not heal today, that healing has passed away, or that He only heals on an occasional basis. This is impossible because He has revealed that one of His names is Healer.

"I am the Lord who heals you" (Exod. 15:26), or, "I am the Lord your *Healer.*"

The names of God represent who He is, His unchanging nature and character. He was, is, and always will be our Healer. My name is Derek. That means I am Derek every day of my life. I am not Derek on Mondays, and some other name on Tuesdays! Derek is who I am continually. Likewise, it is not just that God heals on special occasions; He is by His very name and nature, our Healer every day. Our faith must be based on the name, the revealed character of God. He is our faithful, unchanging, loving Healer!

Moreover, *Yahweh Rophe*, the Lord our Healer, is a covenant name of God. It is who He is to us through our covenant with God established on the blood of Christ. This is confirmed by the fact that God revealed Himself as our Healer in the context of the bitter waters of Marah that were healed by a specific tree that God showed to Moses, who then cast it into the waters (see Exod. 15:22-26). God was saying that He was and is our Healer and that He heals through a *tree*.

Two thousand years ago, God cast His Tree into the bitter (sick) waters of humanity. Christ died on the Tree of Calvary and soaked up all sin and sickness into Himself and released the sweet waters of healing to us. The foundational revelation of God our Healer confirms healing is in the atonement, and thus it is available to all, just like forgiveness.

Healing is a good thing and our loving, heavenly Father desires to give us good things, but we must have the confidence in His goodness to come to Him and ask and receive them from Him.

> **Ask** and it will be **given** to you; seek, and you will find; knock, and it will be opened to you. For everyone who **asks receives**, and he who seeks finds, and to him who knocks it will be opened. Or what man is there among you who, if his son asks for bread, will give him a stone? Or if he asks for a fish, will he give him a serpent? If you then, being evil, know how to give **good gifts** to your children, **how much more** will your Father who is in Heaven **give good things** to those who **ask Him!** (Matthew 7:7-11)

Healing is a good thing, so it is included in this promise. Therefore if we ask for healing, it will be given to us. What earthly father would deny healing to his child if it was within his power to give it? How much more our heavenly Father?

But we must be diligent to receive God's words of healing into our heart, for only then will we have the confidence to receive from Him.

*My son, give attention to My **words**; incline your ear to My sayings. Do not let them depart from your eyes; keep them in the midst of your heart; for they are **life** to those who find them, and **health to all their flesh*** (Proverbs 4:20-22).

Getting Healed is designed to lead you step by step through the key truths of God's Word to build your confidence in the Lord as your Healer, enabling you to come to Him and receive your healing. These truths will transform your whole understanding of divine health, enabling you to walk by faith in the healing power of God.

Tricia Patrick, a member of my church who is experienced in the healing ministry, says:

> I believe that if I had not learned the truths Pastor Derek Walker teaches in this book, I would not be alive today. As a fairly new Christian, passionately in love with Jesus, I was convinced healing was for today and I became determined to understand how it worked. I had been healed myself and had seen others healed through prayer, but not consistently. This spurred me on to seek the Lord for a deeper understanding. Over about ten years in Guildford we organized many Healing Conferences that gave us the opportunity to learn different aspects of healing from anointed teachers and healing evangelists. Over time I came to believe that healing was accomplished for us by Jesus just as much as our sins were forgiven. When we moved to Oxford, my faith took further steps forward, as I found the teaching of Pastor Derek most helpful in explaining healing in an especially coherent way. His clear, logical approach leads us step by step toward our goal of being healed.

As you follow along through this book, your expectancy and faith will rise as you discover that *you **can** receive your healing!*

Chapter One

Position Yourself to Receive

I invite you to open your heart and spirit to the healing that God desires for you. Whether physical, emotional, spiritual, or relational, Jesus has already paid the price for your total healing. Getting healed is not for everyone else—it is for you!

PHASE I

This book is designed to teach you how to *believe* you *receive* your *healing*. First of all, you must get into *position* to *believe* you *receive* your healing from God when you pray.

Our key Scripture contains the words of Jesus in Mark 11:24 (KJV):

> *"Therefore I say to you, whatever things you desire* [including healing], ***when you pray, believe that you receive*** *them* [healing], *and you will have them* [healing]."*

Mark 11:24 is a very important Scripture. Jesus gave emphasis to this by introducing it with, "Therefore I say to you," indicating that He means what He says and He will back it up. Therefore we must take it seriously. It tells us how to receive "whatever things you desire " from God. Healing is certainly included in this promise, for we certainly do desire healing, and healing is a good thing that God provides for humankind. Of course, this verse does not apply to healing alone, but also to all our blessings in the New Covenant. So much of our discussion can be applied to receiving the other blessings of God, like wisdom and forgiveness, but we will focus on healing.

Mark 11:24 says that we will have what we ask for if we believe we receive it when we pray. Therefore we must attain the position of faith where we can believe we receive the answer when we pray.

PREPARATION

There is diligent preparation required to reach this position of faith which involves gaining some vital knowledge of God from studying His Word. This book is designed to help you in this preparation, by giving you the key truths you need to be in position to obey Mark 11:24 and *believe you receive* your healing when you pray.

Mark 11:24 describes what we are to do from the human-side of things. It tells us:

Desire + Pray + Believe you receive = You will have them.

Notice that results are not promised to those who just desire them, or to those who just pray for them, but to those who also *believe* they *receive* them when they pray. First of all, we must obviously desire healing (God will not give it to us against our freewill). Then, if we desire healing we must pray (ask God for it). This is the first principle of faith. God is the Source. Look to God for the answer, for He is the Source of all healing. Call upon Him and trust Him for healing, for He said, *"I am the Lord your Healer."* Then, when we pray we must also *believe we receive* our healing from God. If you have a problem with these truths, remember Mark 11:24 came from the lips of Jesus Himself.

People usually fail, not because they stop believing they received, but because they had never entered the realm of believing they received in the first place. If we only desire and pray, we are always trying to get God to heal us, which is different from believing we receive healing when we pray. We will then think, talk, and act differently.

KNOWING THE GOD-SIDE

There is a God-side and a human-side to Bible subjects. Both are important, but we must know the God-side first, for it to be possible for us to have the appropriate human-side response. Thus to get into the position of faith where we can believe we receive when we pray, we must have certain God-side information from the Word of God. Before we can implement the human-side (believe we receive), we must first obtain the necessary, foundational God-side revelation.

If we find it hard to believe we receive, it is because this foundation is not yet properly established in us. When it is, it will be easy to enter the realm of believing we receive. The more God-side truth we know, the easier it is to do what God expects of us. When we know the God-side truth, it will be easy for us to fulfill the human-side requirement of believing we receive our healing.

For example: "...love one another [human-side], as I have loved you [God-side]..." (John 13:34). "Husbands, love your wives [human-side] just as Christ also loved the church [God-side]..." (Eph. 5:25). If we do not know how He loved us, it is difficult to obey this command, but when we have a revelation of His love, it is easier to love others.

In leading people to salvation, we must first share the Gospel of what God has done, then call for human-side (faith) response (see Rom. 10:9 and John 3:16). If someone is having trouble obeying Romans 10:9, which says, "that if you confess with your mouth the Lord Jesus and believe in your heart that God has raised Him from the dead, you will be saved," then we need to provide more God-side material. We must teach the God-side (grace) to build their faith to receive and obey, rather than condemning them by telling them don't have enough faith.

Likewise, in order to obey Mark 11:24 and believe we receive our healing, we need to have sufficient God-side truth in us. We will now study these truths from the Word necessary to receive our healing.

Our ability to position ourselves to believe we receive depends on how teachable we are, how committed we are to gain the knowledge of God's Word that we need. Jesus' words in Mark 4:23-25 can be interpreted as saying:

> *If anyone has ears to hear* [the Word] *let him hear. Take heed what you hear. With the same measure* [of hearing] *you use, it* [healing] *will be*

measured to you; and to you who hear, more [healing] will be given. For whoever has [ears to hear the Word], to him more [healing] will be given; but whoever does not have [hearing ears], even what he has will be taken away from him.

The degree of importance that we place upon what we hear determines the quantity and quality of the fruit produced in our lives. Study these truths until you are satisfied with the fruit produced.

Four Steps

There are four successive steps to take—four truths to believe—to reach the position where we can believe we receive healing when we pray. The following four truths lead you to the top level:

Goal Achieved: In a Position
to Believe to Receive
_____

Step IV. Know God's Method
_____

Step III. Know God's Gift
_____

Step II. Know God's Nature
_____

Step I. Know God's Will
_____

To reach the top level where you are in position to believe you receive when you pray, you must take four steps up. We do this by believing four important truths about God, from God's Word.

If these steps are missing, it is very difficult for people to reach the position to believe they receive when they pray, because they don't have the essential foundational knowledge of God necessary to reach it. As we go step by step, we find the next step is within our capability to reach and maintain. But if we don't go step by step, it will seem impossible to reach the position where we can believe we receive when we pray.

These steps can be likened to learning arithmetic. The first step is learning how to add, then the next step of subtraction becomes attainable. Then it is possible to go on to take the next step of learning multiplication and then division. Only when we have taken all these steps are we in the position to calculate fractions. As understanding fractions is out of reach for those who don't know the previous four concepts, so is believing you receive when you pray is out of reach if you have not been given the foundational knowledge of God that you need to reach this position. Being able to believe we receive healing (like calculating fractions) may be a position that seems impossible to reach, but as we go step by step, we will find the next one is within our capabilities to reach and to maintain.

In the next few chapters, each of these steps are examined closely, and you will gain the knowledge of God that empowers you to reposition yourself in the realm of believing you receive when you pray.

What You Must Know

When it comes to believing we receive our healing, there are certain things we *must* know about God. There are things we *should* do and things we *must* do. We should wash our car, but we must put gas in it to be of any use. We should exercise but we must eat to live. Likewise, there are things we *should* believe and things we *must* believe. To receive salvation there are things we *must* believe, "If you confess with your mouth the Lord Jesus and believe in your heart that God has raised Him from the dead, you will be saved" (Rom. 10:9).

The failure is not that people do not believe, but that they do not believe what they *must* believe. Thus we must ask, "What knowledge about God *must* the sick accumulate in order to position themselves to believe they receive their healing?"

Hebrews 11:6 tells us that when we come to God to obtain something from Him, there are two things that we must believe about God in order to please Him and succeed in our request:

> But without faith it is impossible to please Him, for he who comes to God must believe that He is, and that He is a rewarder of those who diligently seek Him.

So this Scripture is saying, Without faith it is impossible to please Him, for he who comes to God (successfully) *must believe that:*

1. He is our Healer today, He wants to heal us, and

2. He is a Rewarder of those who diligently seek Him.

We please God when we come to Him and successfully receive.

This requires *faith*. But what kind of faith is needed to receive from God? It must contain these two essential beliefs about God. Notice that these two *must beliefs* are about the nature of God, not about the problem. There is no problem too big for God!

Thus in coming successfully to God in prayer, it is more important for us to know about God, than it is to fully understand our problem. It is helpful to know something about the problem, but it is essential to know about God. Therefore we must learn to magnify God *over* the problem, seeing it through the eyes of God and His power.

We do not deny our problems, we face them; but we must focus more on God and who He is to us. Therefore we must know more about God than we do about our problems. Many Christians fail to receive from God because they are so preoccupied with the problem that they fail to meditate on God and His Word. They are so caught up with the *problem* that they fail to see and receive the *solution*.

These two beliefs stated in Hebrews 11:6 are not optional beliefs, but beliefs that we must have when we come to Him, "He who comes to God *must believe* that *He is* (our Healer), and that He is a *Rewarder* (a generous *Giver* of healing)."

We are not to come to Him in prayer to see if He is and if He will reward (answer) us. These beliefs must already be well-formed before we even come to Him. These two *must beliefs* give us our first two steps toward the position where we can believe we receive when we pray.

Moreover, notice that *both* of these beliefs are essential, just having one of these beliefs is insufficient. Both of these beliefs must be equally strong in us before we can have the confidence to come to Him and believe we receive.

DILIGENCE AND CONFIDENCE

Hebrews 4:11 tells us that we must show diligence in order to enter this place of rest (in our Promised Land)—the realm of knowing we have possessed the promise by faith, "Let us therefore be diligent to enter that rest, lest anyone fall." We enter in and possess the promise by believing we receive it, but if we are not diligent in the Word, we will fail to enter in because of unbelief. The diligence required is in studying God's Word, for that is where faith comes from: "For the Word of God is living and powerful, sharper than any two-edged sword..." (Heb. 4:12). Initially, Israel failed to enter their Promised Land because of their lack of preparation in and obedience to the Word, resulting in them quickly being overcome by doubts and fears. Forty years later, God told Joshua that his key to success was to meditate in the Word (see Josh. 1:8). It is our diligence to let the Word form our beliefs about God that prepares our hearts to be the diligent seekers of Hebrews 11:6 who are able to please God by coming to Him and *obtaining* (believing we receive) the mercy of healing.

Hebrews 4:16 says:

> *Let us therefore come boldly to the throne of grace, that we may obtain mercy* [for ourselves] *and find* [ministry] *grace to help* [others] *in time of need.*

We can come with confidence, believing that He wants to heal us and that He is the Giver of healing, because it is a throne of grace. Therefore we can come to Him and obtain mercy. Healing is a mercy (see Mark 10:47,51-52), so we are invited to come and obtain healing from God. If we have prepared ourselves in the Word, we will come to God with confidence, knowing that we have full access to God through Jesus (see Heb. 4:14-15), and that He is faithful to His Word and sits on a throne of grace, ready to freely give us healing, because Jesus has already paid for it in full with His blood.

In the next chapter, we take the first step toward the position of being able to receive when we pray, by establishing the first vital truth—God's will is to heal us. Until this belief is firmly established in us, it is clearly impossible for us to believe we receive our healing.

HEALING TRUTHS

- The Lord Jesus Christ Himself said that whatever things you desire (including healing), when you pray, believe that you receive them, and you will have them (manifested). He meant exactly what He said! He told us exactly how to receive our healing from God.

- There are three conditions we must fulfill:

    1. We must *desire* it.

    2. We must *pray* and ask for it.

    3. We must *believe we receive* it when we pray.

    It is on this third point that most people stumble.

- Phase I in obeying Mark 11:24 is *getting into position to believe you receive* your healing when you pray.

- There are four necessary beliefs that must be formed in us from God's Word before we are in position to believe we receive our healing when we pray:

    1. Know God's Will

    2. Know God's Nature

    3. Know God Gift

    4. Know God's Method

Chapter Two

Know God's Will

STEP 1. KNOW GOD'S WILL: HE WANTS TO HEAL YOU

Step 1 toward the position where we can believe we receive our healing when we pray is to know that God's will is to heal us. God wants to give us health. He wants us to be well. We must first of all know *what is God's will*, for faith begins when the will of God is known. God's will for us is healing. His will is for us to be well. He wants to heal us.

God said. "I am the Lord who heals you" (Exod. 15:26). This is His unchanging name and nature, and so He always wants to heal us. This is what Hebrews 11:6 means when it says, "He who comes to God must believe that *He is.*" This must mean more than, He who comes to God must believe that God exists, for then it would just be stating the obvious, especially since the Bible takes the existence of God for granted (see Gen. 1:1), and assumes that man knows this (thus the Bible never tries to prove God's existence), for God has put this in our hearts (see Rom. 1:18-20). Believing *God is* means believing He is a present-tense God, the God of *now*. Thus it's not enough to believe that Jesus *was* the Healer, but that He is our Healer today!

So first of all we must believe and be able to say, "It is God's will to heal me. He is my Healer. His will is for me to be well." When we believe this, we have met the first condition of pleasing God with our faith. We will have taken our first step in the journey toward being in position to believe we receive when we pray.

To encourage you to believe that healing is God's will, I want share with you the dramatic testimony of how God healed my wife, Hilary, in the most unlikely circumstances. She had turned her back on her Christian up-bringing, and had become involved in the occult.

HILARY'S HEALING

For years Hilary searched for truth, but could not find it. Instead, she was increasingly tormented with fearful thoughts. Regular visits to a spiritist medium only left her more afraid. Then she started to feel intense pain in her shoulders and elbows. Her hands started to swell, and she felt as though she had raging toothaches in her shoulders, elbows, hips, hands, and gradually all over her body. The doctor diagnosed rheumatoid arthritis, and prescribed all kinds of drugs to deal with the swelling and the pain. Nothing seemed to work.

Soon she could not even hold a pen in her hand; her parents had to cut up her food and help feed her. She could not hold a cup of tea or answer the telephone because the receiver was too heavy. Not only was it terribly painful to bend her joints, but she also felt she had no power in her hands. The disability was getting worse. Despite heavy doses of drugs, she was in pain 24 hours a day. Moreover, the drugs' side effects included uncontrollable shaking and feeling sick. At night she lay awake, her whole body racked in pain, as though red hot knives were searing through every joint in her body. She tried everything, but nothing seemed to bring lasting relief.

She felt so enclosed in the pain and disability that she wanted to die, but she was afraid of death. Then she met a friend, Jeannie, who told her how she had recently been healed, and that she believed God could heal her too. She invited Hilary to some local healing meetings. But when Jeannie arrived to pick her up on the first evening of the meetings, Hilary did not want to go with her. When Jeannie came back again the next night, Hilary had taken an excessive dose of drugs to ease the pain so that she felt like she was floating. When Jeannie told her father, "We can take her on a stretcher," Hilary responded, "Get that fanatical woman out of here. I don't want to go. Doesn't she realize I'm sick?" But Jeannie persevered and came back on the third evening and was very forthright, "You are going to come tonight. This is your last chance!" Grudgingly, Hilary went with her.

When the meeting started, things went from bad to worse! The songs were so soppy and she was annoyed by the stickers saying, Smile, Jesus loves you! In protest, Hilary refused to sing. She was blocked from leaving by Jeannie sitting at the end of the row. To make matters worse Jeannie said, "By the way, we are Pentecostals!" That was like a dirty word to Hilary. Then when Evangelist Fred Smith spoke, she became very angry because he warned people against the dangers of spiritism, saying that the occult controlled peoples' lives in order to destroy them, and that it was evil and wrong. Hilary was furious. He was talking about her friends! She was so busy being angry that she did not listen to the rest of the sermon. Then she heard him say, "Give your heart to Jesus." Suddenly her anger evaporated, and she knew she had to respond and give her heart to the Lord.

She sensed it was her last chance, for otherwise she would surely die!

After praying for people to receive salvation, Fred invited people forward for healing. When Fred came to Hilary, he looked at her and said, *"God has saved your soul; now He is going to heal your body."* Then Fred placed his hands on her head and commanded a spirit of arthritis to leave her. At that moment, the pain became a hundred times worse. She wanted to scream. Then suddenly the most amazing power came through the top of her head. As this power hit her body, the pain left, and she felt warmth and a sense of well-being flood her whole body. It was a tangible feeling of God's power touching her.

She fell down under this power and lay there for a few minutes. Then Fred helped her to her feet, and said, "In the name of Jesus, raise your arms!" She knew this was impossible. For four months she could only raise her arms a few inches. But as she started to raise them, she found she could raise her arms above her head without pain. All heaviness had gone, and mobility was back in her joints. She could move her arms round and round. She felt incredible joy.

HEALING DESPITE SINS

I want you to notice what an unlikely candidate Hilary was for healing. She admits that her attitudes were so bad, that God should have told her to go away and only come back when she had sorted herself out. But God loved her so much that He still wanted to heal her despite her sins. She identifies with Ephesians 2:4: "But God, who is rich in mercy, because of His great love with which He loved us." God loves you just as much and wants to heal you too!

First John 5:14-15 also describes this first step of confidence in God:

*Now this is the confidence [belief] that we have in Him, that **if we ask anything according to His will**, He hears [answers] us. And if we know that He hears [answers] us, whatever we ask [according to His will], we know that we have the petitions that we have asked of Him [we know that we received it when we prayed].*

Like Hebrews 11:6 this key Scripture in First John gives us the foundational beliefs necessary to put Mark 11:24 into practice. It describes the confidence we must have in God—in His will and character—in order to possess the answer to our prayer. In other words, we need to have certain strong beliefs about God in order to believe we receive the answer. The first confidence that we must have is that we are asking according to His will. Thus if we are asking for healing, we must believe that it is God's will for us, otherwise we will not be able to believe we receive it, and so we will not possess our healing.

The first step toward being able to receive healing or any blessing from God is knowing that it is His will. For example, when we received salvation, the first step we had to take was to believe that it was God's will for us to be saved, that Jesus is our Savior. How can we believe we receive our healing when we pray, and step away from God's throne knowing that we have received it, if we are unsure whether it is even God's will to heal us? How can we believe we receive our healing when someone prays for us, and go away knowing we have it, if we are unsure if healing is God's will?

God's willingness to heal us is clearly the first God-side truth that must be embraced for us to reach the position of believing we receive when we pray. Therefore, the first thing to check with people who are ill is whether they believe this truth. If their faith is weak on this point, they need to receive the Word concerning God's willingness to heal. This belief must be formed and be made strong in us by accumulated knowledge from God's Word. The more supporting Scripture we know, the stronger our faith will be—experiences alone can be misleading and often lead to wrong conclusions.

SCRIPTURE SUPPORT AND TYPES

Proof 1: The Old Testament Types and Shadows Show Us that God's Will for Us Is Healing

Throughout the Old Testament, God provided many prophetic pictures of the coming Messiah and what He would do for us. These types included objects (e.g., Tabernacle), people (e.g., Joseph), rituals (e.g., sacrifices), and events (e.g., Red Sea crossing). They were shadows that revealed the truth of the substance who Christ is (see Col. 2:17).

Type 1. The Bronze Serpent

> *Then they journeyed...and the soul of the people became very discouraged on the way. And the people spoke against God and against Moses.... So the Lord sent fiery serpents among the people, and they bit the people; and many of the people of Israel died. Therefore the people came to Moses, and said, "We have sinned, for we have spoken against the Lord and against you; pray to the Lord that He take away the serpents from us." So Moses prayed for the people. Then the Lord said to Moses, "Make a fiery serpent, and set it on a pole; and it shall be that everyone who is bitten, when he **looks** at it, shall **live**." So Moses made a bronze serpent, and put it on a pole; and so it was, if a serpent had bitten anyone, when he **looked** at the bronze serpent, he **lived** (Numbers 21:4-9).*

As a result of Israel's sin, they were bitten by serpents and were sick and dying. A fiery bronze serpent was set on a pole, and they were told that if a serpent had bitten anyone, when he looked at the bronze serpent, he would live, receive life. All who heard and believed the Word and looked at it *lived*. Thus all who looked on the bronze serpent, trusting in God's provision, would be *forgiven* and *healed* he would live. Thus forgiveness was freely available for all who sinned, and healing was freely available for all who were sick. God wanted them all to be forgiven and healed, and so provided forgiveness and healing for all.

In John 3:14-16, Jesus said that what this serpent did for Israel, He would do for the whole world through His death on the cross. Thus the bronze serpent was a type of Jesus Christ on the cross:

> *As Moses lifted up the serpent in the wilderness, even so must the Son of Man be lifted up that **whoever believes in Him** [looks to Him] should not perish but have eternal life. For God so [in this way] loved the world that He gave His only begotten Son [to die on the cross], that **whoever believes** in Him should not perish but **have everlasting life**.*

Just as all who looked on the uplifted bronze serpent lived, so whoever looks to Christ lifted up on the cross and judged for their sins shall live (have everlasting life).

When the Israelites believed the Word and looked upon the bronze serpent lifted up on a wooden stake, they saw a representation of Jesus dying on the cross for their sins. The serpents are a picture of sin, which contains the poison of sickness and death. When people were bitten by the serpent of sin, they received this poison—the curse of sickness and death—into his being. This was pictured by sinful Israel being bitten by the serpents and becoming sick unto death.

By lifting up the bronze serpent, God was revealing His remedy. The perfect Messiah would be lifted up and would become sin and a curse for us so we could receive righteousness and blessing (see 2 Cor. 5:21, Gal. 3:13-14). He did this by bearing our sin, sickness, and death, so that we could have forgiveness, healing, and life. He received our sin and its poison, including sickness, upon Himself.

The fact that this serpent was bronze signifies that our sin has been judged upon Jesus, for on the cross He received the judgment in our place. Thus the serpent of sin and all it contains—the curse—has been taken by Jesus and defeated once and for all. Those who looked upon the bronze serpent saw their sin and curse, sickness and death, lifted up, judged, and defeated, and as a result they received spiritual and physical life—forgiveness and healing.

What God did for Israel through the bronze serpent lifted up on the pole, He did for all the world through Jesus lifted up on the cross:

> *Christ has redeemed us from the curse of the law having become a curse for us, (for it is written: "Cursed is everyone who hangs on a tree"), that the **blessing** of Abraham might come upon the Gentiles in Christ Jesus, that we might receive the promise of the Spirit through faith* (Galatians 3:13-14).

The curse includes every kind of sickness (see Deut. 28). All sickness is in the curse! Therefore, Christ has redeemed us from the curse of sickness, for He became accursed with sickness for us, so that the blessing of healing might come upon us, being made freely available to us for us to receive. He bore our sicknesses and carried our pains, so that through His wounds healing is ours to receive, see Isaiah 53:4-5. He redeemed us from sickness and released life and healing to us.

How then can we possibly doubt that it is God's will to heal us?

As Israel **looked and lived**, so likewise all who *look*, trust, upon Jesus dying for their sin and sickness on the cross will receive *life*—forgiveness, healing, and eternal life. They will *live!* They will receive both spiritual and physical life in abundance. Thus it must be God's will for all to be forgiven and healed. If healing is in the Type, how much more must it be in the fulfillment.

Type 2. The Passover Lamb

> *Your lamb shall be without blemish, a male of the first year. ...Now you shall keep it until the fourteenth day of the same month. Then the whole assembly of the congregation of Israel shall **kill** it at twilight. And they shall take some of the **blood** and put it on the two doorposts and on the lintel of the houses where they eat it. Then they shall **eat the flesh** on that night; roasted in fire, with unleavened bread and with bitter herbs they shall **eat** it. Do not eat it raw, nor boiled at all with water, but roasted in fire—its head with its legs and its entrails. You shall let none of it remain until morning, and what remains of it until morning you shall burn with fire. And thus you shall eat it: with a belt on your waist, your sandals on your feet, and your staff in your hand. So you shall eat*

*it in haste. It is the Lord's Passover. For I will pass through the land of Egypt on that night, and will strike all the firstborn in the land of Egypt, both man and beast; and against all the gods of Egypt I will execute judgment: I am the Lord. Now the **blood** shall be a sign for you on the houses where you are. And when I see the **blood**, I will pass over you; and the plague shall not be on you to destroy you when I strike the land of Egypt* (Exodus 12:5-13).

...indeed Christ, our Passover, was sacrificed for us (1 Corinthians 5:7).

What the Passover Lamb did for all of Israel, Jesus did for all people through His sacrificial death on the Cross:

1. The blood of the Passover Lamb protected them from curse and judgment; it provided forgiveness of sin. Applying the blood to their house is a picture of us trusting under the blood of Christ for our forgiveness and deliverance from judgment.

2. The Body of the Passover Lamb provided health and strength. Eating the Lamb is a picture of us receiving by faith the healing that comes through the sacrifice of Christ. They all ate the Lamb, and they all received strength and health for their journey; "He also brought them out with silver and gold, and there was none feeble among His tribes" (Ps. 105:37).

3. The blood of Jesus was shed for our forgiveness and salvation.

4. His body was broken for our physical healing and well-being.

In Communion we take:

1. The *wine* representing His *blood*, shed for the *forgiveness* of our sins.

2. The *bread* representing His *body*, broken for our *health*, strength, healing, and sustenance for the journey of life.

As God set the children of Israel free to be able to go forth in health and strength to serve and worship Him, so by His blood He has set us free from sin, so that we can go forth and serve and worship Him in freedom from fear. Likewise, He wants us to have all the health and strength that we need for our journey of faith through this world, so He has provided it through the broken Body of Christ, the Lamb of God. As God provided a lamb for the healing of every person in Israel, so He has now provided the Lamb of God for the healing of every believer today. It is now up to us to eat, receive by faith, the healing in God's Lamb. Therefore we can conclude from the Exodus and the Passover Lamb that it must be God's will to heal us.

All who ate the Lamb were healed. If God provided healing for all in the type of the Passover Lamb, how much more must He have provided healing for everyone in the fulfillment, the atonement of Christ, the ultimate Passover Lamb, sacrificed for all. If Christ died to provide healing for all, then surely it is God's will to heal you.

His intent is confirmed by the prophecy of the Messiah as God's ultimate sacrificial Lamb in Isaiah 53. He goes as a Lamb to the slaughter (see Isa. 53:7) bearing all our sicknesses and pains (see Isa. 53:4), and through His wounds healing is released, given, to us (see Isa. 53:5). Those who believe this Report of the Lord (the Gospel) will experience His healing power (see Isa. 53:1).

Proof 2: The Words of Jesus Reveal the Father's Will

Jesus claims that His Father was in perfect agreement with His words (see John 14:10, 12:49). When a leper said to Jesus, "If You are willing You can make me clean." Jesus replied, "I am willing, be cleansed" (see Mark 1:40-43). Jesus did not stop and pray to ask God if it was His will to heal him. He knew it was the Father's will to save and heal everyone. Thus it is God's will to heal us today. He is no respecter of persons, and He does not change. What He will do for one, He will do for all.

There were three commissions of Jesus to three groups of people (to the 12, to the 70, and finally to the whole Church). To all three groups, He gave a commission to heal the sick. He authorized, empowered, and commanded them to heal the sick. He gave no restrictions or qualifications limiting who may benefit. He did not hint that they should pray to check if it was God's will to heal a certain person, because His will is to heal everyone.

The three commissions of Jesus:

1. "He called His twelve disciples together and gave them power and authority over all demons, and to cure diseases" (Luke 9:1). "He gave them power...to heal all kinds of disease" (Matt. 10:1).

2. In Luke 10:1,9, He "appointed seventy others also, and sent them," telling them to, "heal the sick there." The implication is they were to heal all the sick.

3. In Mark 16:15-20, He said: "Go into all the world and preach the gospel to every creature. ...In My name...they will lay hands on the sick, and they shall recover."

If healing was not God's will for all, then why would Jesus tell His disciples to heal all the sick every time He commissioned them and sent them out? Why would He give them healing power to heal all kinds of sicknesses and instructions explaining how to minister it if He did not want all people healed? His words consistently show it must be God's will to heal all. Has He changed His attitude? No! "I am the Lord, I do not change..." (Mal. 3:6). "Jesus Christ is the same yesterday, today, and forever" (Heb. 13:8).

Proof 3: The Actions of Jesus Reveal God's Will

Jesus was and is the will of God in action (see John 14:9). When we see Jesus in action, we see the Father working with and through Him. He revealed through His actions that it is God's will to heal all people. With all the multitudes He ministered to, we always see Jesus "heal them all." He never turned away one person, never told anyone that it was not God's will or time to heal them.

Examples:

Jesus went about all Galilee...healing all kinds of sickness and all kinds of disease among the people...they brought to Him all sick people who were afflicted with various diseases and torments, and those who were demon-possessed, epileptics, and paralytics; and He healed them (Matthew 4:23-24).

The implication is that He healed them *all*.

...He cast out the spirits with a word, and healed all who were sick, that it might be fulfilled which was spoken by Isaiah the prophet, saying: "He Himself took [all] our infirmities and bore [all] our sicknesses" (Matthew 8:16-17).

Jesus went about all the cities and villages...healing every sickness and every disease among the people (Matthew 9:35).

When Jesus went out He saw a great multitude; and He was moved with compassion for them, and healed their sick. He healed all their sick (Matthew 14:14).

Mark 5:24-34 describes a woman with an incurable flow of blood:

When she heard about Jesus, she came behind Him in the crowd and touched His garment. For she said, "If only I may touch His clothes, I shall be made well." Immediately the fountain of her blood was dried up, and she felt in her body that she was healed of the affliction. And Jesus, immediately knowing in Himself that power had gone out of Him, turned around in the crowd and said, "Who touched My clothes?" But His disciples said to Him, "You see the multitude thronging You, and You say, 'Who touched Me'?" And He looked around to see her who had done this thing. But the woman, fearing and trembling, knowing what had happened to her, came and fell down before Him and told Him the whole truth. And He said to her, "Daughter, your faith has made you well. Go in peace and be healed of your affliction."

Although this was the healing of an individual, it happened in such a way that showed that the healing power of God upon Jesus was available for all, and if His healing power was for all, then it must mean it was God's will to heal all. The way she received her healing proves that God is willing to heal all, for anyone could have received the same way as she did. In fact, in Luke 6:17-19, Mark 6:53-56, and Matthew 14:34-36, we see many people come to Jesus for healing in the same way, and they were all healed.

You see, the woman did not ask Him for her healing, but came from behind and took healing power from Him, receiving His commendation, not condemnation. She could do this, because she had heard of Jesus preaching the Good News that He was anointed to heal the sick, and that this healing power was upon Him and available for all (see Mark 5:27).

Luke 4:18-21 records what Jesus preached wherever He went, "The Spirit of the Lord is upon Me, because He has *anointed* Me…to *heal* [all]…to set at liberty [all] those who are oppressed; to proclaim the acceptable year of the Lord.…" The Acceptable Year of the Lord was the Year of Jubilee—a time of grace and restoration for everyone.

In the ministry of Jesus, we see the perfect will of God in action. He healed *all* who came to Him for healing:

> God **anointed** Jesus of Nazareth with the **Holy Spirit and with** [heal-ing] **power** who went about doing good and **healing all** who were oppressed of the devil, for God was with Him (Acts 10:38).

God richly anointed Jesus with the power to heal everyone who was oppressed by sickness, so it must be God's will to heal all people, for He has not changed. "Doing good" speaks of a wealthy man giving generously to those in need. Thus, Jesus freely distributed the healing power that God had given Him to all those who needed it. He went about giving this power to anyone who needed and wanted it, and it delivered them all from the oppression of sickness.

When people failed to receive healing, Jesus never put this down to a lack of willingness on God's part to heal them—as often happens today. Instead, He was upset because God's will, healing, was not being accomplished on earth as it is in Heaven. He was shocked and amazed, because He knew God wanted to heal them and that God had provided abundant power for them to be healed. His reaction in these cases confirms that healing must always be God's will.

When He could do no mighty works of healing at Nazareth, He did not blame God, but marveled at their unbelief, which prevented them receiving. He responded by teaching the Word to build faith in the people (see Mark 6:5-6). In other words, it was not a failure on God's part to give healing, but a failure on the part of people to receive it.

When His disciples failed to deliver and heal an afflicted boy (see Mark 9:17-29 and Matt. 17:14-21), Jesus was clearly distressed by the unbelief present. This time the problem was mostly with the disciples who had failed to heal the boy, and He responded to this situation by correcting their failure and immediately healing him. Someone who saw the initial failure of the disciples to heal him might have easily deduced that it was not God's will to heal this boy, but they would have been totally wrong, as Jesus demonstrated.

Proof 4: The Plan of Redemption Scriptures

The Scriptures that reveal what Christ accomplished through His death and resurrection show that He purchased both spiritual and physical salvation for us—forgiveness and healing. What Jesus did on the cross, He did for all people, so these benefits must be available for all. Thus healing is for all, as well as forgiveness! If, when Jesus died on the cross, He paid the full price for the forgiveness and healing of all people, then it must be God's will to heal everyone.

Isaiah 53:3-5 is a prophecy of what the Messiah would accomplish in His death and resurrection:

> *He is despised and rejected by men, a Man of sorrows and acquainted with grief* [literally: sickness]. *And we hid, as it were, our faces from Him; He was despised, and we did not esteem Him. Surely He has borne* [as a burden] *our griefs* [sicknesses] *and carried* [away from us] *our sorrows* [pains]; *yet we esteemed Him stricken, smitten by God, and afflicted. But He was wounded for our transgressions, He was bruised for our iniquities; the chastisement for our **peace*** [shalom, which means health and wholeness in spirit, soul and body] *was upon Him, and by His stripes we are **healed*** [literally: healing is to us].

Thus, healing is for us and it flows to us because of His stripes (wounds). (Isaiah 53:10 adds: *"He has put Him to grief,"* which literally means He has made Him sick.

He was made sin with our sin, so that we might be made righteous with His righteousness (2 Cor. 5:21). Likewise, He was made sick with our sicknesses, so we might be made healthy, whole, with His health.

Matthew 8:16-17 confirms that this prophecy refers to Jesus Christ and the healing that He provided for all of us on the cross:

> [Jesus] **healed all** who were sick, that it might be fulfilled which was spoken by Isaiah the prophet, saying: "He Himself took [all] our infirmities and bore [all] our sicknesses (Matthew 8:16-17).

Likewise, First Peter 2:24 says: "who Himself bore our sins in His own body on the tree...by whose stripes you were **healed.**"

These Scriptures prove that God provided healing for all humankind through Christ's death. This proves His willingness to heal all. *All* means you too! Therefore God's will is to heal you also.

The atonement is the basis for the fulfillment of Psalm 103:2-4:

> Bless the Lord, O my soul, and forget not all His benefits: who forgives all your iniquities, **who heals all your diseases**, who redeems your life from destruction, who crowns you with lovingkindness and tender mercies (Psalm 103:2-4; see Mark 10:47,51).

The benefits, blessings, of God were all provided through the cross. These include healing from all sicknesses, as well as forgiveness from all sins—for on the cross Jesus died for all our sicknesses and sins. We must remember *all* His benefits and forget none of them. It is not enough to acknowledge His forgiveness, but ignore His healing. We must remind ourselves from God's Word that through the cross, God has provided healing for all our sicknesses. If God forgives all our sins, then forgiveness must always be His will for us. If God heals all our diseases, then healing must always be His will for us too. We are told not to forget any of these benefits of the Lord, but rather think about them, receive them, and thank God for them. The Church has obeyed this for the benefit of forgiveness, but many have forgotten and even denied the benefit of healing.

Proof 5: The Character of God

God's will for His people is always healing, for God is love. Surely if we believe He is love, we also must believe He wants to heal us. What loving father wants his children to be sick? Yet our heavenly Father loves us even more (see Matt. 7:9-11). Thus God will always give the bread of healing to His beloved children when we ask for it (see Matt. 6:11), for healing is the children's bread (see Matt. 15:26).

> *The Lord is good to **all**, and His tender mercies are over **all** His works* (Psalm 145:9).

Healing is a mercy (see Matt. 20:30-31), so this verse in Psalm 145 could read: The Lord is good to all and His compassionate healings are over all His people.

We have now established the scriptural basis for *the first belief that we must have*, in order to reach the *position* of being able to believe we receive our healing when we pray: *God's will is always to heal His people*. In order to reach this position of faith, and then maintain it, we must become and then re-main confident that it is always God's will to heal us, for He is our Healer.

God's desire for us to be in good health is clearly expressed in apostle John's inspired prayer, "Beloved, I pray that you may prosper in all things and be in health, just as your soul prospers" (3 John 2). As your soul pros-pers in the Word, you will be in position to believe you receive healing, and so maintain your body in good and proper health.

We have seen that the proof of this is revealed throughout the Bible, from the Old Testament revelations of God to Israel that typify our salva-tion in Christ, to the words and works of Christ and His atonement where He bore our sins and sicknesses, and the promises of God that confirm healing is ours on the basis of the atonement. Thus God has given us full confirmation that He wants to heal us, so we might have the confidence to come to Him to receive our healing.

If you now believe that God's will is to heal you, you have taken your first step toward the position of being able to believe you receive your heal-ing when you pray, and you are now ready to take the next step.

Now that you have the confidence that healing is always God's will, you must maintain this confidence by continuing to meditate on the truths that support this belief. When doubts come that attack this belief, speak these Scripture truths out loud, declaring, *"It is God's will to heal me."* This will cause the doubts to retreat so you will find it easy to remain true to your belief that healing is God's will. This is what Jesus did. When He was attacked by thoughts that opposed God's will, He responded by saying: "it is written..." (Matt. 4:4,7,10). This is using: "the Sword of the Spirit, which is the word of God" (Eph. 6:17). The "word" here is *rhema* in the Greek, which refers to a spoken word. We must put the word of God onto our lips, and then it becomes a sword that the Spirit uses to break the power of the evil one.

We overcome satan by our words testifying to the blood of the Lamb: "They overcame him by the *blood* of the *Lamb* and by the *word* of their testimony..." (Rev. 12:11).

Therefore, we must study the Scriptures that support the belief that God's will is to heal us, so that we:

1.   Know and embrace this belief.

2.   Share it with others.

3.   Defend it using these truths.

HEALING TRUTHS

- *The first step* toward the position of being able to receive our healing when we pray is to know that *healing is God's will.* This foundational belief must be established in our hearts by God's Word.

- The Bible is clear that *God wants to heal us.* He is our Healer.

- There are five proofs pointing the way toward the position of receiving our healing:

  — *Proof 1:* The Old Testament Types and Shadows, including the bronze serpent, the Passover Lamb, and the waters of Marah.

  — *Proof 2:* The *words* of Jesus reveal God's will to heal us.

  — *Proof 3:* The *works* of Jesus reveal God's will to heal us.

  — *Proof 4:* The Plan of Redemption Scriptures proves that healing is in the atonement. This means it must be God's will for us.

  — *Proof 5:* The character of God reveals God's love for His children, which means He does not want us to be sick. He wants to show us mercy.

Chapter Three

Know God's Nature

Therefore I say to you, whatsoever things [including healing] *you desire,* **when you pray,** **believe** *that you* **receive** *them* [healing] *and you will have them* [healing] (Mark 11:24 KJV).

GOD IS A LIBERAL GIVER OF HEALING

Because God is a liberal giver of healing, this means that we will have what we ask for, if we believe that we receive it when we pray. How can we get into the position of faith, whereby we can believe we receive healing when we pray?

There are four successive steps that we must take, which are necessary to reach the position where we can believe that we receive healing when we pray. Each step involves the establishment in our heart of an essential belief about God that He has revealed about Himself in His Word. Once these beliefs are firmly established in us, we will be in position to easily and confidently believe we receive when we pray. When we pray and believe we receive, we enter the realm of knowing that we possess the answer, for then we have the confidence that we received it when we prayed. This in turn gives us the confidence that we will *have them* (see the manifestation).

We have now taken step 1 toward the position of being able to believe we receive our healing when we pray: *God's will is to heal us.*

Goal Achieved: In a Position
to Believe to Receive
_____

Step IV. _____

Step III. _____

Step II. _____

Step I. Know God's Will *(Healing is God's will for me)*
_____

We saw in Hebrews 11:6 that when we come to obtain something from God, there are two things that we *must believe* about God in order to please Him and succeed in our request (receive the answer):

Without *faith* it is impossible to please Him, for he who comes to God *must believe* that:

1. *He is a Healer.*

2. He is a *Rewarder* of those who diligently seek Him.

These beliefs must be well-formed before we even come to Him. These two *must beliefs* give us our first two steps toward the position where we can believe we receive our healing when we pray.

As mentioned previously, first we must believe that *God is our Healer* today (see Exod. 15:26). We must believe it is definitely God's will to heal us, for He is and always will be our Healer. But there is something else we *must* believe, if we want to receive our healing:

STEP 2. KNOW GOD'S NATURE: HE IS A LIBERAL GIVER OF HEALING

If we are to believe we receive healing from God when we pray, it is not enough to know that healing is God's will, but also that God's *nature* is to give it freely to us upon request. Therefore, we must also know the answer to the question, What is God like? We must know His nature. Someone may generally want us to be healed, but not necessarily be able or ready to give it to us as soon as we ask for it. We know of course that God has the power and resources to heal us, but does He freely give us healing upon request, or does He sometimes delay giving us healing for a time, withholding it from us? Does He wait until we are worthy or until we give Him something in return, or do something for Him? Is He quick or slow to give? Is He a liberal Giver, or does He lack the desire or love to heal us when we pray?

Hebrews 11:6 tells us that in order to please God when we come to Him, the second thing we must believe is that God is a Rewarder, a Giver, not a withholder. We must believe that He cares enough to immediately respond to those who come to Him. In other words, we must believe that God is a generous *giver* of healing. He does not give grudgingly, He gives willingly and liberally. He delights to give and bless us. To please God, we must come to Him believing that:

1. It is His will to heal us.

2. He will freely give healing to us when we pray.

We must *believe in Him*, that is, in His character, His nature of love and goodness toward us. We must not just believe that He desires us to be healed, but that His actions are consistent with His desires, so that He will give us healing when we ask.

If we do not believe in Him, that is, in His generosity, then we can neither please Him nor believe we receive anything from Him.

How can we believe we receive anything unless we believe He gives it to us upon approach and request? Believing we receive it when we pray requires us to believe that He gives it to us when we pray. Thus if God expects us to believe we receive it when we pray, then it means that He promises to respond immediately and give it to us. The fact God expects us to believe we receive it when we pray means that He must be ready to respond immediately and give it.

As we go through these four steps to reach the highest level, let's keep track of the questions and answers that move us along:

> Step 1: What is God's will? God's will for us is healing and health.

Step 2: What is God like, what is His nature? God is a liberal Giver. He answers us when we pray according to His will, giving to us liberally, richly, and freely, without delay.

God is not reluctant, grudging, complaining, hesitating, withholding, or delaying; He has plenty to give and is full of love and willingness to give. He is love. He gives lavishly. He is gracious and gives freely. He is rich and gives richly. He is all powerful and is a liberal, quick Giver of healing power. He does not hold back from us, but gives us life and healing freely and abundantly (see John 10:10).

Each step makes the next one reachable. If we have Belief 1 (Healing is His will), then Belief 2 (He is a liberal Giver) will follow easily. If we know that healing is His will, then it is a simple next step to knowing that upon approach He will never say to us: No or Wait awhile. Otherwise there would be something lacking in God's goodness, for on the one hand He would want us healed, but on the other hand, He would be slow to give us healing. He would then be double-minded. If we believe that about Him, then we are double-minded and inconsistent in what we believe about God and His character and we will fail to please Him! (See James 1:5-8.)

Step 2 follows easily from Step 1. If we know it is His will to heal us, then we can be sure He is ready to give it when we ask, because by nature He is not a withholder, but a Giver of healing.

HAVE CONFIDENCE

First John 5:14 makes this very point:

*Now this is the **confidence** that we have **in Him** that if we ask anything according to His will, He hears us.*

This verse assumes that we are asking for something—like healing—that is according to God's will, something He wants us to have. (How can we know if something is God's will? His will is His Word!) It tells us we can be confident that when we ask for it, He will hear us. This means more than God being aware of our prayer, for He knows all things. It actually means that He answers the prayer, He responds and sends the answer to us immediately! Thus we can know, be sure, that when we ask for healing, God will give us healing.

The basis of this confidence is the character of God, *"this is the confidence that we have in Him."* If He wanted to heal us, but failed or delayed in giving us healing, then there would be something lacking in His goodness and love toward us. But we know He is perfect, and so we know He will give us healing, or anything else that is according to His will, when we pray.

Once we have the confidence that healing is God's will, it logically follows, from His gracious and generous loving nature, that we can have the confidence that He will hear us when we pray, which means He responds and sends the answer—healing—to us immediately.

Clearly the first step of confidence that we need to believe we receive is knowing that we are asking for something according to His will. If we are not asking for something that is His will for us, then He is not going to give it, and our prayer will fail—we have no right to receive it. If we ask for something according to God's will, but we are not sure that it is His will for us, then although He will give it to us, we will not be sure that He is giving it to us and so we will not have the confidence to receive it—we will not be able to receive it. First of all, we must be confident that it is God's will to heal us. Then we can also be confident that God will hear and answer us when we pray for healing by giving, releasing, healing to us.

First John goes on to say that if we have this confidence in God—that He is a liberal Giver of healing—then we can approach Him with confidence to believe we receive our healing when we pray:

> *And if we know that He hears* [answers] *us, whatever we ask* [according to His will], *we know that we have the petitions that we have asked of Him* [we know that we received it when we prayed] (I John 5:15).

In conclusion, First John 5:14-15 tells us:

1. We must know that healing is according to God's will.

2. We must know that God is a liberal Giver of healing who hears and answers us when we pray by immediately giving us healing.

3. We then will be in a position of confidence to believe that we receive the answer (healing) when we pray, so that as soon as we have prayed, we will know that we possess (have) the answer, for we will know that when we prayed God gave it and we received it.

These same two beliefs, or steps, were necessary when we came to Christ to receive salvation—forgiveness and eternal life:

1. We had to believe that He is the Savior; He wanted to save us.

2. We had to believe He would save us upon request, giving us forgiveness and life when we ask for it.

When we prayed to receive Christ, believing these two things, our faith pleased Him (see Heb. 11:6), and we succeeded in receiving His free gift of eternal life. Now we can walk the path of Hebrews 11:6, for every child of God initially came to Him this way.

This is not an unfamiliar path; you have already walked the path of believing He is the Savior and that He is a Giver of Salvation upon request. You can learn to walk the same path with healing, by believing He is the Healer, and that He is a Giver of healing upon request, coming to Him.

However in the area of healing, many come with the first belief alone—God generally wants to heal me, but He might not do it now—but that is insufficient. Salvation and healing were supplied through the same sacrifice, so God wants us to be healed just as much as He wants us to be saved. Why do we judge Him quick to give salvation to all who call on Him (see Rom. 10:13), but slow to give healing to the sick? We must not only believe in His willingness to heal, but also in His generosity as a Giver, in giving us healing liberally, abundantly, freely, and richly when we come and ask Him.

When we deeply believe and trust in these two beliefs, we are qualified to come to God in prayer in a way that pleases God according to Hebrews 11:6:

Without *faith* it is impossible to please Him, for he who comes to God *must* believe that:

1. He is the Healer.

2. He is a Rewarder of those who diligently seek Him—we must believe He is a Giver not a withholder of healing.

In coming to God, we must have these two beliefs established in our hearts, which requires us to diligently seek Him by studying His Word. These beliefs must be well-formed in us through our diligence in His Word, before we even come to Him. We will then have the kind of faith that pleases God by successfully obtaining our requests, receiving our reward from Him. *He is a Giver to all who ask, but a Rewarder only to the diligent; for they alone believe they receive the reward.*

If we see a person in the Bible who came to Jesus and received healing and a commendation from Him for his faith, then we can be sure that the person pleased God and thus believed according to Hebrews 11:6. Jesus, in His response to them, perfectly reveals God's nature; see John 14:9. Therefore, we should see that they had the two key beliefs, which we have been discussing.

Let us consider some of these examples from Jesus' ministry, and follow their examples of faith.

1. Mark 5:24-34. The woman with the issue of blood received her healing and was commended for her faith. Before she came to Jesus she clearly believed: (1) He was willing and able to heal her, and (2) that He would freely give her healing the moment she came to Him to obtain it, by touching the hem of His garment.

2. Luke 7:1-10. The centurion's faith was commended, and he got his answer. He had Belief 1 as shown by sending the first group with the message: "Come and heal him." Belief 2 is seen in his sending the second group with the message: "Speak the word only and he shall be healed."

3. Luke 5:17-26. Jesus saw their faith as the paralytic and his friends came through the roof and was pleased, for He did not discourage their efforts. The paralytic received his healing. Their actions certainly showed a Hebrews 11:6 faith.

We have seen that these two beliefs are vital to pleasing God and for getting us into position to believe we receive from Him. Therefore they need to be strongly formed in us by a diligent study of God's Word.

So let us now look at the scriptural support for Step 2.

Scripture Support and Types

Proof 1: God Is a Liberal Giver

*If any of you lacks wisdom, **let him ask of God, who gives to all liberally** and without reproach, and it will be given to him. But let him **ask in faith, with no doubting,** for **he who doubts** is like a wave of the sea driven and tossed by the wind. For let not that man suppose that he will receive anything from the Lord; he is a **double-minded** man, **unstable in all his ways** (James 1:5-8).*

I believe this Scripture passage could be interpreted as follows: If any of you lacks wisdom (or healing), let him ask of God, who *gives* to *all liberally* and without reproach (withholding the answer), and it will be *given* to him. But let him ask in faith (believing that God is a liberal Giver), with no doubting (differing from the fact that He is a liberal Giver), for he who doubts (differs) is like a wave of the sea, driven and tossed by the wind. For let not that man suppose that he will receive anything from the Lord. He is a double-minded man, unstable in all his ways.

This passage tells us how to receive healing from God. We must simply ask God for it, and He will surely give it to us. But we must ask *in faith,* or else we will fail to receive what God has given.

God always faithfully gives the answer to us upon request: "Let him ask of God and it will be given to him," but we will not necessarily be in the position of faith to receive what He has given to us. In order to receive God's answer, we must *ask in faith.* This implies there is something we must believe when we pray.

James tells us that it is essential that we believe something about God without any doubting, holding on to a different belief that opposes what God's Word reveals, or else we will certainly fail to receive our answer from God. So what are we told about God in verse 5 that we must believe in order to receive our answer?

"Let him ask of God who gives to all liberally and without reproach and it will be given to him." This truth supplies the essential knowledge we need about God's character in order to pray in faith, believing we receive the answer when we pray. We must ask in faith believing that: "God gives to all liberally." We must believe God is generally a liberal Giver of healing to all who come to Him; and therefore, He will surely give (healing) to us in particular. Thus we must believe that our God is a liberal *Giver*, not a withholder. He is not reluctant or hesitant in responding. He does not delay. He is the God of all *grace*, the God of *immediate response*.

We must become persuaded by God's Word of both His will and His grace; that healing is His will for us, and therefore He gives it to us liberally. To doubt means to differ, to hold a differing or opposing opinion. We are not to differ from this truth in our minds by allowing differing thoughts to gain a foothold. Thus when we ask God for healing, we must not differ, disagree, with the truth of His Word that God is a liberal Giver, who answers us with healing as soon as we pray for it. If we have opinions and beliefs that differ from His Word on this issue, then we are questioning His goodness and cannot please Him. Moreover, our hand of faith will be paralyzed by these doubts, so we will be unable to receive the healing that God faithfully gives us upon request. When we ask for healing, we must believe in God's goodness and refuse to differ with the truth that God gives (healing) to all liberally.

We must allow ourselves to become fully persuaded by diligent study of God's Word that He is by nature a liberal Giver who will freely give us the healing we need without delay, so nothing in us will oppose this belief, or doubt this truth, and thus prevent us from trusting completely in the goodness and grace of God to heal us.

With God's Word, we can pull down any strongholds of unbelief in us and bring every thought into subjection to Christ (see 2 Cor. 10:4) so that none of our thinking will differ with the truth of His Word, that God is a liberal Giver. Then we will be able to come to Him in faith (trusting in His generous nature toward us, not doubting that He is a liberal Giver to all, but knowing He will freely give the answer to us upon request) and believe that we receive our healing when we pray.

James 1:7 describes a man who fails to receive from God: "Let not that man suppose that he will receive anything from the Lord." It is not that God does not send the answer to him, but that he is unable to receive it. Why? His doubting, disagreeing, or differing with God's Word, which says that God is a liberal Giver, prevents him from asking in faith and believing he receives his healing.

What prevents him from being able to receive from the Lord? The answer is in verse 6: He differs, contends, argues, or struggles with something concerning God in his thoughts. To see what this is we need to go back to verse 5 where we are told something about God that is essential for the person to believe: "God gives [healing] to all liberally, without reproach." If we are to please God, we must believe this. If we do not believe God will give to us the healing we need when we ask for it, then we do not believe this, and as a result we will fail to believe we receive our healing when we pray, so that we will receive nothing from the Lord.

If anyone has beliefs about God that differ from His Word on this issue of His generosity, this Scripture tells us that person will be unable to receive anything from the Lord, for doubts paralyze. Our failure to believe that God gives to all freely prevents us from receiving anything from the Lord—for we will doubt if God will give it to us.

James 1:8 says, "he is a double-minded man, unstable in all his ways." This person is in two minds. His thinking about God is divided and undecided; he is not fully persuaded by God's goodness. He has faith to pray, but not to receive. He looks to God as his Source, but doubts His supply. He lacks (healing), and believes that God has his answer (Belief 1), but he does not believe that God will necessarily give it upon request (Belief 2) and so differs from the truth that He is a Rewarder, Giver. This way of thinking is inconsistent and double-minded. This instability in his beliefs and thoughts will show up as instability in his life (see James 1:8). As a result, he does not have the confidence to receive from God (see James 1:7), and being unable to hook up successfully to God's power, he will be like a wave tossed to and fro by problems and sickness (see James 1:6).

We have seen Hebrews 11:6, James 1:5, and First John 5:14 all say that a person must pray with confidence in God, believing that He is a liberal

Giver. If we differ from this belief, then we will not "please Him" or "receive anything from Him" or "have His petitions."

Proof 2: God Is a Rich Giver

> *...the same Lord over all is **rich to all** who call upon Him. For: "whoever calls on the Name of the Lord shall be saved"* (Romans 10:12-13).

The word *salvation* includes healing as well as all the riches of His grace, so this verse in Romans could be interpreted as, "whoever calls on the Name of the Lord for healing shall be healed from the riches of His grace."

> *Blessed be the God and Father of our Lord Jesus Christ, who has blessed us with every spiritual blessing in the heavenly places in Christ. In Him we have redemption through His blood, the forgiveness of sins, according to the riches of His **grace** which He made to **abound** toward us in all wisdom and prudence* (Ephesians 1,3,7-8).

God is not only *rich*, but He also gives *richly, abundantly*, to us. He does not hold back; he gives the riches of His grace freely to us. Jesus said:

> *I have come that they might have **life**, and that they might have it more abundantly* (John 10:10).

Sickness is part of the curse of death, but healing is part of the blessing of life. Therefore Jesus came that we might have healing. *Jesus is the abundant Giver of health—life!* Abundance describes fullness of life. It is His life poured out so that it is more than you can contain, like a river overflowing its banks. God gives to us richly without holding back.

> *For the Lord God is a sun and shield; the Lord will give grace and glory; no good thing will He withhold from those who walk uprightly. O Lord of hosts, blessed is the man who trusts in You!* (Psalm 84:11:12)

As a sun, He radiates healing power. As a shield, He protects us from sickness. The Lord freely gives us the grace and glory of healing, and no good thing (including healing) will He withhold from us as we walk in fellowship with Him. Therefore the person who trusts in Him will be blessed with healing.

The Lord is my Shepherd; I shall not want. You prepare a table before me in the presence of my enemies; You anoint my head with oil; my cup runs over. Surely goodness and mercy shall follow me all the days of my life... (Psalm 23:1,5-6).

Since the Lord is my Shepherd, I shall not want for healing. God has prepared a banquet table full of blessings for me to eat as much as I want. On the table is healing, the children's bread (see Matt. 15:26). Surely the mercy of healing shall follow me all the days of my life.

*Command those who are rich in this present age not to be haughty, nor to trust in uncertain riches but in the living God, who **gives us richly all things** to enjoy. Let them do good, that they be rich in good works, ready to give, willing to share, storing up for themselves a good foundation for the time to come, that they may lay hold on eternal life* (1 Timothy 6:17-19).

God "gives us richly all things to enjoy." Surely healing and health are good things that we enjoy. Therefore God gives us healing richly, abundantly. He is a *rich Giver* of healing. From His riches of health, He freely and richly gives us healing.

Here Paul, the writer of First Timothy, asks the rich to transfer their trust from their riches to "the living God." Since he was asking them to do this, he had to give them some information about the One in whom he wanted them to put their trust. So in order to encourage them in this, Paul tells them about the character of God, saying that He is both *rich* and a *rich, generous Giver* of all blessings. Therefore they can safely put their trust in the unchanging God as their Provider, rather than in uncertain, transitory earthly riches.

Paul also points to God's nature as their example. For as God is both *rich* and a *rich Giver* to those in need, so these *rich* men are to show their faith by being rich in good works, ready to give richly to others, willing to share their blessings richly. Thus Paul is calling them to (1) *trust* in God as One who gives to them all things richly, and (2) *follow* His example of generosity in using their riches to bless people and meet their needs.

*Grace and peace be multiplied to you in the knowledge of God and of Jesus our Lord, as His divine power **has given to us all things** that pertain to life and godliness through the knowledge of Him, who called us by glory and virtue, by which have been given to us exceedingly great and precious promises that through these you may be partakers of the divine nature (2 Peter 1:2-4).*

Again we see God's rich generosity toward us, for by His power He has given us all things that we need in this life. This surely includes healing. He holds nothing back from us, but it is up to us to partake of His grace—to come to Him and believe we receive what He has given to us and freely offers to us. We can only do this through the knowledge of God, of His nature and His promises. We are to partake of (receive) the divine nature (of health and healing) by knowing His great and precious promises of healing. When we know from His Word that He is a liberal Giver of healing, we can come to Him and partake of His healing. In this way, His free gift of healing, His grace, increases in our lives through the knowledge of God and His provision in Christ.

Acts 10:38 summarizes His healing ministry and confirms that His nature was to richly give healing to the sick, upon request: "God *anointed* Jesus of Nazareth with the Holy Spirit and with [healing] *power*, who went about doing good and *healing all* who were oppressed by the devil, for God was with Him."

The healing anointing on Jesus was not for Himself, but for others. He freely received it in order to freely give it away to those in need. This is the meaning of: "He went about doing good." In First Timothy, Paul was describing a man who is so rich, that he goes around liberally giving away his money to every worthy cause or need. Acts 10:38 tells us that God anointed Jesus with healing power, and that He was so rich in this healing anointing that He went about freely and richly distributing it as a free gift to all who needed and wanted it, with the result that all the sick were healed. He did not withhold healing from anyone, but gave it to them upon request. In doing this, He perfectly revealed the will of God who never changes. Thus God's will is for all to be healed, and He still richly gives us His healing power through Christ, when we come to Him and ask for it.

Proof 3: God Is a Free Giver

. . .God is love (1 John 4:8).

. . .I have loved you with an everlasting love. . . (Jeremiah 31:3).

Giving is the very nature of Love.

*Christ **loved** the church and **gave** Himself for her* (Ephesians 5:25).

If God is love, He must be a Giver:

*God so **loved** the world that He **gave** His only begotten Son. . ."* (John 3:16).

God is our loving Father. The nature of a godly father is to give (see 2 Cor. 6:18).

*God so **loved** the world that He **gave** His only begotten Son that whoever believes in Him should not perish, but have eternal life* (John 3:16).

God gave His Son to die for us that we might be able to receive His life.

God's love means He does not want us to perish in spiritual or eternal death or physical sickness. It was the revelation of God's loving and giving nature that enabled us to come to Him and believe we receive eternal life. We must continue to believe that God is a Giver, who gives liberally, richly, and freely, all the more now that we are His children! If God did not give freely to us, but held back some good things from us—perhaps because we are not worthy—then surely He would have held back from giving us His most valuable and costly gift—His only Son whom He gave up to die for us, so that in Him we would have all things:

*He who did not spare His own Son, but delivered Him up for us all, how shall He not with Him also **freely give us all things?**"* (Romans 8:32)

If God so loved us that He gave His Son to die for us, to purchase and make every blessing available to us, will He not also with Him freely give us all things, including healing? How could we think He would say to us No or Not yet if we ask Him for healing? If God loved us so much that He did not even withhold His Son from us, would He withhold His healing from us?

Surely not! He freely gives us all things! This includes healing. Therefore, He freely gives us healing. He does not hold it back from us (see Rom. 5:10).

In fact in giving us His Son, He also freely gave us all things, for it was through His death and resurrection that they were purchased for us and provided to us. So now they freely come to us in, through, and with Christ. Thus along with Christ, God freely gives us healing.

Since God freely gives us all things, James 4:2 concludes that "you do not have because you do not ask." If we do not have healing, it is not because of His reluctance to give it. This Scripture implies that when we ask, He gives the answer freely. I believe that if we lack something, the problem is not in His giving, but in our asking and receiving.

I believe Matthew 7:7-12 could be interpreted as such: Ask (for healing) and it (healing) will be given to you. For everyone who asks (for healing) receives (healing). The answer is always Yes, not No, or Wait, let me think about it. Or what man is there among you who, if his son asks for *bread* (healing is the children's bread, see Matt. 15:26) will give him a stone (leaving him hungry, waiting for the healing that he needs). If you then, being evil, know how to give good gifts to your children, how much more will your Father who is in Heaven (immediately) give good things (healing) to those who ask Him! (We would give healing at once to our children because we love them, so how much more will our heavenly Father give healing at once to His beloved children when we ask for it, for His love is so much greater than ours). Therefore (just as God in His love freely gives us on request the good things we need) whatever you want others to do to you, do also to them for this is the Law (of God's Love).

We are told to walk by the same Law of Love that God lives by. If you were sick, you would want someone with your healing to give it to you without delay. Therefore the Law of Love, by which God lives, dictates that if anyone, including God, possesses healing power, he should give it to the sick person immediately upon request.

What would you think of a father who has food for a hungry son, but withholds it when his son requests it? What would you think of a father who has healing for his son, but withholds it, when his son requests it (either by delaying giving it or not giving it at all for some mysterious reason)? Yet people think God is like that concerning healing! In Matthew 7:7-12, Jesus rebukes this stinking thinking:

> *Ask, and it will be given to you; seek, and you will find; knock, and it will be opened to you. For everyone who asks receives, and he who seeks finds, and to him who knocks it will be opened. Or what man is there among you who, if his son asks for bread, will give him a stone? Or if he asks for a fish, will he give him a serpent? If you then, being evil, know how to give good gifts to your children, how much more will your Father who is in heaven give good things to those who ask Him! Therefore, whatever you want men to do to you, do also to them, for this is the Law and the Prophets.*

God is ready to give healing to us. Of course, we must come to God and ask Him for it, but when we do, God freely gives healing to us:

> *Let us therefore come boldly to the throne of **grace**, that we may **obtain mercy** and find grace to help in time of need* (Hebrews 4:16).

To come boldly is to come to God with confident faith that He wants to heal us and that He will freely give to us the mercy of healing upon request. Thus we are told to come and obtain healing from God, whenever we need it.

Likewise, Mark 11:24 invites us to come to God, believing we receive our healing, taking it by faith, when we pray. God must be offering it to us freely, holding it out for us to come and get it, for we are told not just to come and ask for it, but to come and obtain—believe we receive—it.

In order to obey Hebrews 4:16, we are to go away from the throne with the healing in our hands! The throne to which we come is the throne of *grace*, because of the blood of Christ. Therefore, God must be offering us *healing* as a *free gift*, and will *freely*, immediately, give it to us when we ask for it.

We have now seen the scriptural support that shows us that God is a *liberal, rich, free Giver* of *healing*, who gives us healing without delay when we ask for it. If this were not true, we would have no right to believe we receive healing when we pray. Moreover, if we do not believe it to be true, we would not be able to believe we receive healing when we pray. Therefore it is essential to have this belief from the Bible firmly established in our hearts.

HEALING AND ATONEMENT

One key knowing this aspect of God's nature is to also realize that healing is in the atonement.

In Step 1 we saw proof that healing, as well as forgiveness, is provided to us on the basis of the atonement—Jesus' death on the cross. Christ died for all, bearing all our sins and sicknesses, so we could all be forgiven and healed. When Jesus died, He declared, "It is finished" (John 19:30) meaning the price is paid in full. Jesus has fully paid the price required for our full salvation (spirit, soul, and body). If healing was not in the atonement, then Jesus would have told a lie, for He would have only paid in part.

This proves that healing is God's will for us all (Step 1). The atonement also proves Step 2, that God is ready to give us healing when we ask for it, healing is available from God upon request, just like forgiveness. The atonement means that in one sense God has already given it to us. On the cross, Christ paid the price in full for our healing and forgiveness, and thus He put healing to our account, so that it is ours—it belongs to us in Christ, "by His stripes we are healed," (Isa.53:5) or *healing is ours.*

Thus the completed atoning work of Christ explains the following verses which describe every blessing, including healing, as having already been given to us by God. These same verses provide some of the best proof of God's generous nature—that He is a liberal Giver, withholding nothing good from those who ask Him:

> Ephesians 1:3: *Blessed be the God and Father of our Lord Jesus Christ, who has blessed us with every spiritual blessing in the heavenly places in Christ.* "In Christ" signifies that it is through His death and resurrection.

> Second Peter 1:3: *His divine power has given to us all things that pertain to life and godliness* [through His death]. All these blessings are purchased by His blood.

First Corinthians 2:12: *We have received...the Spirit who is from God, that we might know the things* [including healing] *that have been freely given to us by God.* These things, including healing, are ours through Christ's death.

Although people might be undependable, being double-minded and undecided about fulfilling their promises and plans, God is not this way or He would be guilty of unfaithfulness:

"But as God is faithful, our word to you was not [sometimes] *Yes and* [sometimes] *No. For the Son of God, Jesus Christ, who was preached among you by us—by me, Silvanus, and Timothy—was not* [maybe] *Yes and* [maybe] *No, but in Him* [through His death and resurrection] *it has always been Yes. For all God's promises* [including His promises of healing] *of God in Him are Yes, and in Him Amen, to the glory* [healing manifestation] *of God through us* (2 Corinthians 1:18-20).

If God's promises are all Yes! in Christ (not maybe or later), then He cannot withhold healing from us, but must be ready to freely give healing when we ask Him. He wants His glory, healing, to shine through us so that in Christ, through His death and resurrection, He has confirmed all His promises of healing to us with a final Yes!, and sealed it with His blood. Then when we believe His promise that He freely gives us healing, adding our Amen to it (I believe I receive it, that now settles it, it is established), then His promise of healing comes to pass through us—our faith in Him.

He who did not spare His own Son, but delivered Him up for us all, how shall He not with Him also **freely give us all things?** (Romans 8:32)

God won't withhold healing from any of us, for in giving up Jesus to die for us, He also gave us all things with Him, through His death. Jesus died for us that we could have all things, including healing. He now freely gives us all things, because through giving up Jesus to die for us, every blessing was purchased for us and made available to us. Thus He did not just give us Christ, but also all things, including life and healing, with and in Christ (see 1 John 5:11-12).

So He now offers us healing as a free gift. God's giving nature of love is revealed by the cross, and can now be fully expressed toward us because of the cross of grace. Through the propitiation, sacrifice of Christ where God's justice against us was satisfied, He is free to move in mercy, healing, toward us and pour out every blessing upon us; He has already done so in Christ.

Healing, which is "the children's bread" is ours (see Matt. 15:26). It belongs to us, for it has already been given to us on the basis of the cross. It has now been put on the table ready for us to eat (see Ps. 23:5). Now it is just up to us to come and receive it, for now in Christ, through His death and resurrection, it is available to us upon request. God will not deny or withhold from us, or delay giving us something that He has already paid for and has offered to us as a free gift. Thus Jesus told us to pray, "Give us this day our daily bread" (Matt. 6:11). In other words, He invites us to come to Him in faith, saying: "I believe I receive my healing now."

Imagine you buy a big box of chocolates, enough for your whole family, and then you tell them it is theirs as a free gift from you, because it is completely paid for, and all they have to do is come to you and receive whatever they want from the box. You are offering it to them as a free gift, available upon request. Being true to your word, you will give it freely, instantly, to anyone who believes your word, and comes to you to receive it. Likewise our healing was purchased on the cross, and released to us in the resurrection, so now we just have to come to God, believing we receive it, and He will give it to us.

It is like this with the spiritual blessings like forgiveness and healing, that God has already given us in the atonement. This is why all the promises of God in Him (through His death and resurrection) are Yes, and in Him Amen (see 2 Cor. 1:20). If we know healing is already given to us in the atonement, then it will be easy to believe God will freely give it to us when we ask Him.

Therefore the Scriptures you read about previously, teaching healing in the atonement (see Isa. 53:4-5, Matt. 8:16-17, 1 Pet. 2:24), not only prove that healing is God's will, but that He has already given it to us through the cross and, therefore, it is available upon request.

Galatians 3:13-14 also teaches us that healing is in the atonement:

> *Christ has redeemed **us** from the **curse** of the law, having become a **curse** for **us** (for it is written, "Cursed is everyone who hangs on a tree"), that the **blessing** of Abraham might come upon the Gentiles in Christ Jesus, that we might receive the promise of the Spirit through faith.*

On the Cross, Jesus redeemed us from the *curse*. Every kind of sickness is under the curse (see Deut. 28:15,61). Therefore Jesus has redeemed us from all sickness, paying the price to set us free from its power. This resulted in the *blessing* of *healing* being released to us in Christ, through His resurrection life. Therefore the *blessing* has *come upon us* through the Holy Spirit, so we might simply *receive* it through faith. This confirms God gives healing freely.

THE RIVER OF LIFE

Jesus says to us: It is done! It is all paid for. I am the Alpha and the Omega, the Beginning, Source, and the End. I will *freely give* of the fountain of the *water of life* to anyone who thirsts—asks (see Rev. 21:6). This water—river—of life contains healing and flows from the atoning sacrifice of the Lamb:

> *He showed me a pure river of **water of life**, clear as crystal, proceeding from the throne of God and of the Lamb...on either side of the river was the tree of life... the **leaves** of the tree were for the **healing** of the nations. [Therefore] let him who thirsts come. Whoever desires, let him **take** the water of life freely (Revelation 22:1-2,17).*

The leaves contain healing virtue, which they receive from the river of life. Therefore the river contains healing power and those who are thirsty for (desire) healing are invited to come to God's river and take (drink) the healing water freely (receiving it as a free gift by faith).

All are invited to come and take, receive by faith, what has already been poured forth, given, to us through Christ. This river of life and healing in the Spirit flows freely to us from God the Father through the sacrificial Lamb, the Son, who has risen from the dead. It represents God's free giving to us of His life and healing, flowing to us in and by the Spirit, on the basis of the cross of Christ.

> *How precious is Your lovingkindness, O God! Therefore the children of men put their trust under the shadow of Your wings. They are abundantly satisfied with the fullness of Your house, and You give them drink from the river of Your pleasures* (Psalm 36:7-8).

God provides abundant riches to those who trust in Him.

The Gospel message is that salvation—forgiveness and healing—has been paid for and is therefore now freely available to all as a gift. The Good News that the disciples were told to preach was, "The kingdom of heaven is *at hand*" (Matt. 10:7). This means forgiveness, eternal life, and healing are at hand. *At hand* means God has freely given it to us, so we just have to reach out and receive it with the hand of faith.

The Gospel is not just that God wants to save and heal us, but that through Christ, salvation and healing has already been freely given to us, for us to freely receive. The disciples were told to preach this message and confirm it by healing the sick, "Heal the sick. ...Freely you have received, freely give" (Matt. 10:8). They had been freely given healing power, it was entrusted to them in Matthew 10:1. Now the disciples were to heal the sick by freely giving through the healing power they had been given. If healing was given freely to the sick before the cross, how much more now!

THE TYPES

The Types described in Chapter 1 also confirm healing is in the atonement, that healing is God's will, and that it is God's nature to freely give healing.

Previously we saw that Type 1, the bronze serpent, and Type 2, the Passover Lamb, show that healing is God's will, seeing that He has provided it for all on the basis of the atonement.

Both of these types or pictures of Christ, and His Salvation, also reveal that through the atonement, healing is freely available for anyone to come and receive it, so that it is immediately given to us on request. Since healing, like forgiveness, is in the atonement, it means that healing has already been given, and so is available now on request.

In Type 1, as soon as they believed the word, promise, and *looked* in faith at the bronze serpent, a symbol of the cross, they *lived*, they received their healing. Healing power life was given to them freely on the basis of the cross, so when they asked for it by looking to the cross, it immediately flowed into their bodies.

In Type 2, as soon as they ate the Passover Lamb, which had been sacrificed for them, they received strength and health for their journey. Thus through the Lamb, physical healing was freely available to all. When they partook of it, they immediately received healing.

Type 3: The Waters of Marah (Exodus 15:22-26)

> *Moses brought Israel from the Red Sea; then they went out into the Wilderness of Shur. And they went three days in the wilderness and found no water. Now when they came to Marah, they could not drink the waters of Marah, for they were bitter. Therefore the name of it was called Marah. And the people complained against Moses, saying, "What shall we drink?" So he cried out to the Lord, and the Lord showed him a tree. When he cast it into the waters, the [bitter] waters were made sweet [healed]. There He made a statute and an ordinance for them, and there He tested them, and said, "If you diligently heed the voice of the Lord your God and do what is right in His sight, give ear to His commandments and keep all His statutes, I will put [allow or permit] none of the diseases [to come or remain] on you which I have brought [allowed to come] on the Egyptians. For I Am the Lord who beals you"* [or I am the Lord your Healer] (Exodus 15:22-26).

Here God reveals His unchanging name, nature, as "I *am* the Lord your Healer." He demonstrated this eternal, universal truth by healing all of Israel from a sickness through a *tree* that soaked up all the bitterness (sickness) in the waters (of humanity) and made them sweet, releasing healing. This is a type and picture of the cross where Jesus bore our sicknesses and gave us healing. It is in this context that God reveals Himself as our Healer, showing that He heals us through the tree, the atonement of Christ. This Type teaches that on the basis of the cross, His nature as a free Giver of healing is manifested to all humankind, so that He now freely gives us healing.

God's revealed nature, name: He *is now our Healer!*

Type 4: The Year of Jubilee (Leviticus 25:8-18)

You shall count 49 years. Then you shall cause the trumpet of the Jubilee to sound on the 10th day of the 7th month; on the Day of Atonement you shall make the Trumpet to sound throughout all your land. And you shall consecrate the 50th year, and proclaim liberty throughout all the land to all its inhabitants. It shall be a Jubilee for you; and each of you shall return to his possession, and each of you shall return to his family (see Lev. 25:8-10).

> *In this Year of Jubilee, each of you shall return to his possession* (Leviticus 25:13).

The Jubilee was good news to the poor, a special year of grace, forgiveness of debts, release from slavery, and restoration of everything, any land and houses, that had been lost. These blessings were released on the basis of the atonement, for it began on the Day of Atonement, a type or picture of the sacrifice of Christ. The atonement and the Jubilee were for all. Therefore the Jubilee trumpets were sounded everywhere, declaring that these purchased blessings were now freely available from God as a free gift, because the atoning sacrifice had been accepted by God.

All who heard and believed the Jubilee trumpet proclamation could immediately claim their forgiveness, liberty, and full restoration by faith, and receive these blessings without delay. In order to receive the blessings of Jubilee, a man had to believe the proclamation that the sacrifice had been slain, the price was paid in full, and therefore the purchased blessings were now released freely to him, for him to receive. Believing this, he would then be able to claim—believe he received—them, knowing that as soon as he requested them, they would immediately be given to him. If this is true of the Jubilee blessings of the Type, how much more is it true of the Jubilee blessings of the fulfillment in Christ!

The Jubilee was a picture of the Great Jubilee, that Messiah, the Anointed One, would establish and proclaim on the basis of His sacrifice, in which God would restore everything humankind had lost in the Fall, including spiritual life, righteousness, health, peace, and joy.

Isaiah prophesied this coming Jubilee of Messiah:

> *The Spirit of the Lord God is upon Me, because the Lord has anointed Me to preach good tidings to the poor; He has sent Me to **heal** the broken-hearted, to proclaim **liberty** to the captives, and the opening of the prison to those who are bound; to proclaim the acceptable [Jubilee] year of the Lord and the day of vengeance of our God; to comfort all who mourn, to console those who mourn in Zion, to give them **beauty** for ashes, the **oil of joy** for mourning, the garment of **praise** for the spirit of heaviness; that they may be called trees of righteousness, the planting of the Lord, that He may be glorified* (Isaiah 61:1-3).

Notice the blessings of this Great Jubilee of the coming Messiah included *healing* for all the sick and brokenhearted, the proclaiming of *liberty* of all those held captive and oppressed by sickness, the *restoration* of life, beauty, and joy, for all those under heavy burdens of sorrow, sickness, and pain.

When Jesus came, He declared He was the promised Messiah now come to fulfill this Great Jubilee. He was proclaiming the Year of Jubilee, sounding the Jubilee (Gospel) Trumpet.

> *...And when He had opened the book, He found the place where it was written: "The Spirit of the Lord is upon Me, because He has anointed Me to preach the **gospel** to the poor; He has sent Me to heal the broken-hearted, to proclaim liberty to the captives and recovery of sight to the blind, to set at liberty those who are oppressed; to proclaim the acceptable year of the Lord."...And He began to say to them "**Today**, this Scripture is fulfilled in your hearing"* (Luke 4:17-21).

This is the summary statement of His message: Today, I am fulfilling the Year of Jubilee! You can go free today! You can receive your healing today!

The Gospel is the proclamation of the fulfillment of *Jubilee*.

The Gospel message is the Good News of Jubilee. Jesus went about *teaching* on many different things, but wherever He went, He *preached* the same Gospel message:

> Jesus went about all the cities and villages, **teaching** in their synagogues, **preaching the gospel** of the kingdom, and **healing** every sickness and every disease among the people (Matthew 9:35, see also Acts 10:36-38).

The Gospel message He preached is summarized in Luke 4:18-21. He proclaimed everywhere, in the tradition of the Jubilee trumpeters, that the Jubilee blessings, including healing, were now freely available to all. The healing anointing was now upon Him, so that if anyone believed the Gospel, they could come to Him and receive their healing, for it would be given to them upon request (this *now message* is the very nature of the Jubilee proclamation).

The woman with the issue of blood, mentioned previously, is an example of one who heard and believed this proclamation that healing was at hand. She came from behind and took (believed she received) her healing:

> When she heard about Jesus, she came behind Him in the crowd and touched His garment. For she said, "If only I may touch His clothes, I shall be made well." Immediately the fountain of her blood was dried up, and she felt in her body that she was healed of the affliction. And Jesus, immediately knowing in Himself that [healing] power had gone out of Him, turned around in the crowd and said: "Who touched My clothes?" (Mark 5:27-30).

From His preaching, the woman expected to receive healing as soon as she touched Him. His Word proved true, for instantly healing power flowed from Him to her. The way she received showed that healing was "on tap," available to anyone who came to Him to receive, take, it as she did. So in a sense it had already been given to anyone who wanted it. Jesus commended her faith, confirming that His will was to heal her and His nature is a liberal Giver of healing.

Other examples of many people receiving the same way (see Matt. 14:34-36, Luke 6:17-19) prove that this was no special case.

When Jesus ministered healing, people were either instantly healed or at least their recovery began at once. He told us to expect the same when we pray for the sick (see Mark 16:18). This confirms that God still gives healing at once. Today, it is still the Jubilee (Acceptable) Year of the Lord.

On the basis of Christ's atoning death, it is God's Jubilee time for the whole world, to which He is offering salvation, forgiveness, and healing to *all* as a *free gift* to be received by faith.

This is why He has told us to go preach the Gospel—the Good News of Jubilee Grace—to every creature (see Mark 16:15-20).

> *He says: "In an acceptable time I have heard you, and in the day of salvation I have helped you." Behold,* **now** *is the accepted time; behold,* **now** *is the day of salvation* (2 Corinthians 6:2).

The Gospel is the message of Jubilee for all people. It proclaims that the atoning sacrifice has been made, the price has been paid, and therefore the blessings of salvation are here for us *now*, to come and receive. We have seen that healing was included in the atonement and in the Jubilee Gospel that Jesus preached, which we are still to preach today. Therefore, God will freely release healing to us upon request, for the essence of the Jubilee message is that *today* is the day of salvation (healing) for us. Just come believing and receive.

It is by preaching the Gospel that we sound the Jubilee trumpet, proclaiming that through the death of Christ, forgiveness and healing are now freely available to all. So anyone who hears the Jubilee trumpet can claim forgiveness, healing, and liberty by faith.

The fact that the Gospel is the fulfillment of Jubilee means that God does not withhold any healing from us; He gives it liberally on request, without delay, for it is already ours in Christ.

A SIGN OF HIS PRESENCE

Often God confirms His promise of sending healing immediately by giving a sign of His presence when we ask for healing, such as a feeling of heat. Often people fall down, overwhelmed by His tangible presence upon them. Sometimes He gives an instant manifestation through a gift of healing. These are given to demonstrate His love for us, and to encourage us to believe and trust in God as our Healer.

One Sunday, Paul, a member of our church, came forward for healing prayer for diabetes and its serious complications in his liver and pancreas. The next Sunday there was another call to come forward for prayer, but as he believed the message of receiving God's healing power at the point of prayer, he was reluctant to go forward again for healing since he gone forward the previous Sunday. But his wife, Caity, urged him to go forward for a blessing, and so he did.

Soon after I prayed over him, he became confused by all the strange noises that he could suddenly hear. He realized that God had done an instant miracle in opening his left ear! He was hearing in stereo for the first time in ten years, for he had lost all hearing in it and the doctors had told him it was permanent. Since that day his hearing has been absolutely fine, and he has had no more vertigo or migraine headache attacks. I believe this gift, manifestation of the Spirit was an outward sign to him that God was also healing his internal organs.

Indeed, he has experienced much internal healing in his liver and pancreas since then. Due to several attacks of pancreatitis, his pancreatic function had ceased, both endo and exocrene functions. This left him requiring supplementary digestive enzymes and insulin. His pancreas has regenerated "miraculously," in the words of his consultant doctor! When Paul told him it was interesting he should say that because he had received this miracle through prayer, the doctor answered that he was only speaking metaphorically. Paul can now also produce insulin.

If we know that God is a generous, liberal Giver who loves us passionately and releases healing to us upon request without delay, this will make all the difference when we approach Him. It will change the way we approach Him for healing. It will give us confidence to come to Him *believing we receive* our healing.

BELIEVING WE RECEIVE

We already have this confidence when we come to God on the basis of First John 1:9 to receive forgiveness for our sins: "If we confess our sins, He is faithful [to His Word] and just [through His blood] to forgive us our sins and to cleanse us from all unrighteousness."

We know, on the basis of His blood and His promise, that God's will is to forgive us, and that He freely gives forgiveness to us without delay, when we ask for it. So having prayed, we know from His Word we are forgiven, even if guilty feelings linger. When we ask for forgiveness, He answers and forgives us at once, but we may still feel guilty. Then we have a fight of faith to believe the Word that we have received forgiveness, even though we may still feel condemned.

We can have the same confidence in believing we receive our healing. Having prayed, we can know that we have received His healing power, even if symptoms of sickness remain for a time.

We should say, "Thank You Father, that by the blood of Jesus You have purchased my full salvation and forgiveness. You are totally satisfied by the blood of Jesus, so when I asked for forgiveness, You gave it to me freely. I accept Your forgiveness."

When we finally feel forgiven is not when we are forgiven; God gave it to us when we prayed. Healing works the same way! God always gives it when we pray. But, according to Mark 11:24, there is often a time period between the prayer and the manifestation, so we may still feel unwell. God is Spirit, and He sends the answer in the Spirit, as a spiritual blessing, to be spiritually received by faith.

It then goes to work in our bodies to heal us. We must continue to believe we have received His healing power, declaring our faith that it is working in us. Then the healing, which God has already given us by His grace when we prayed, will be fully manifested in us.

We have discussed many Scriptures to convince us of the two beliefs that we need to fulfill Hebrews 11:6. We must not only be persuaded that healing is God's will for us, this by itself may just indicate a passive disposition of the will, but also that God is actively giving healing to us, for us to receive. He is a liberal Giver of healing.

After we have these beliefs, we must also use these scriptural truths to defend them when doubts arise by speaking out what we know about our God who is a loving and liberal Giver, causing the doubts to retreat, and making it easy for us to remain loyal to our beliefs.

We should also share the truths that support these important and essential beliefs with others, so they too can believe God is a liberal Giver. It is easy to persuade others when our beliefs are firmly established within us from the Word of God.

HEALING TRUTHS

- Step I toward the position of being able to receive our healing when we pray is to know that healing is God's will.

- Step 2 is to know God's nature: He is a liberal Giver of healing. God is a loving, good, generous Giver. He gives freely upon request.

- First John 5:14-15 says that if we have these two foundational beliefs in place, then we can believe we receive (possess) the answer when we pray. Thus First John 5:14-15 gives us the foundation for Mark 11:24.

- Fundamental truths to believe about God:

  - God is a liberal Giver.

  - God is a rich Giver.

  - God is a free Giver.

  - God is a Rewarder not a withholder.

  - God responds immediately.

- Healing is in the atonement (see Isaiah 53:4-6,10; Matthew 8:16-17; I Peter 2:24; Galatians 3:13-14). Therefore healing, like forgiveness, has been purchased by the blood of Christ and available upon request.

- Types of Christ that confirm healing is in the atonement:

  1. Bronze Serpent

  2. Passover Lamb

  3. Waters of Marah

  4. Year of Jubilee

Chapter Four

Know God's Gift

STEP 3. KNOW GOD'S GIFT: GOD GIVES US HEALING POWER

Therefore I say to you, whatsoever things you desire [healing], *when you pray* [for healing], **believe** *that you* **receive** *them* [healing], *and you will have them* [healing] (Mark 11:24 KJV).

We are considering how we can get into position to put Mark 11:24 into practice and receive our healing. To obey Mark 11:24 and believe we receive our healing, we must first know some truths about God. As each belief is formed and established in our hearts by the Word of God, we take another step toward the position of faith where we can believe we receive our healing when we pray—these truths also apply to receiving other spiritual blessings in the New Covenant that are bought and paid for by the blood of Jesus.

So far we have the first two Steps in place:

Step 1: Know God's Will: He wants to heal us.

Step 2: Know God's Nature: He is a liberal Giver of healing.

Goal Achieved: In a Position
to Believe to Receive

Step IV.

Step III.

Step II. Know God's Nature *(God gives without delay)*

Step I. Know God's Will *(Healing is God's will for me)*

Now we are ready to go on to Step 3: Know God's Gift: He gives us healing power when we ask Him for healing.

Step 3 answers the question: What does God give to people in need of healing? Answer: God's gift is His *healing power.*

The Steps so far covered: God's Will, His Nature.

So far, Steps 1 and 2 have covered God's will, we know what His will is, and God's nature, we know what He is like, and now we are about to discuss Step 3, God's gift of healing power. A quick review reveals that:

1.   God's will is to give us healing,

2.   God's nature is to freely give us healing upon request,

3.   God's gift to the sick is His healing power.

The third Step is to recognize and understand what His gift is. We must know what God gives. This might seem obvious, but a lack of understanding of *what* God gives those who are in need of healing when hands are laid upon them, is a big reason why many fail to step into the position of believing they receive when they pray, and become disappointed. This is due to a lack of Bible knowledge concerning what God gives to those in need of healing.

MANIFESTATION OF HEALING

God is Spirit, and so God's way is to give us a spiritual blessing, which goes to work in us producing physical results. Although He sometimes gives us the gift of a miracle manifestation, His normal way is to give us a promised blessing, which we receive by faith.

We can either hope to be healed by an instant manifestation initiated by God, or we can initiate our healing by believing we receive healing power when we pray. If we think that we can only be healed by an instant manifestation, then we will never be able to receive healing by faith. But if we know that God gives us healing power upon request, then it is easy to believe we receive it when we pray—even without feeling anything. God's healing power will then go to work in us to drive out all sickness and affect a recovery.

What do people seek to receive from God when they come to Him for healing? If we are honest, most think that whenever God heals, He gives an instant healing manifestation, and so they quickly check themselves to see if it has happened. Then if nothing seems to have changed when they pray, they deduce that God did not hear (answer) their prayer. If there was no instant manifestation, they deduce that God did not give them anything and go away disappointed. As a result they fail to receive the healing that God gave them.

Although God does sometimes give manifestations of healing to the sick, they are only as the Spirit wills (see I Cor. 12:7-11). It is not what God normally gives. It is impossible to believe we receive an instant manifestation when we pray, for we have no scriptural basis or right to do this. God never promises to give us an instant manifestation when we pray. Therefore we cannot receive an instant manifestation by faith on the basis of Mark 11:24.

Receiving healing through a gift or manifestation of the Spirit has nothing to do with believing we receive our healing. Sometimes, in special cases, God led Jesus to initiate a healing through the gifts of the Spirit, but in that case the recipient was not required to believe they received their healing. Normally, however, once people heard the Word, they initiated their healing by coming to Jesus and believing they received it from Him.

If God only gave healing in the form of manifestations of the Spirit, then why would He tell us to believe we receive our healing (see Mark 11:24)? We would have no need to believe we received our healing—this would be completely unnecessary. The fact that God tells us to believe we receive our healing means that we will not necessarily get an instant manifestation. By all means we can desire and pray for a manifestation, but we cannot presume on this happening. But we can always believe we receive our healing.

Now we are talking about coming to God and believing we receive our healing. When we do this, we are obeying the Lord Jesus when He said in Mark 11:24, "Whatsoever things you ask, when you pray, believe that you receive them [healing] and you will have them" [healing].

We can see that God tells us to believe we receive when we pray—for something that is according to His will, like healing, which was paid for by the blood of Jesus—promising us that if we do we "will have it," or see it come to pass. If God requires us to believe we receive when we pray, we can be sure that God will always give the answer to us when we pray, otherwise how can we possibly receive it when we pray? So, He will give us healing when we ask for it, but we are not to look for, or depend upon, getting an instant manifestation, for we will not normally get one.

Moreover, if we are only looking for an instant manifestation, this will impede us in our receiving healing by faith, for we will immediately check to see if the healing has manifested. Then if there is no instant manifestation, we will conclude that our prayer failed, that it did not work.

It is clear that Mark 11:24 is not talking about believing we receive an instant healing manifestation when we pray. This is confirmed by the language of Mark 11:24 that implies there is normally a time delay between the prayer of faith and the full manifestation of healing; the promise is that if you *believe you receive them, then you **shall** have them*—future tense.

Mark 11:24 tells us that if we would believe we receive when we pray, then (later) we will have (see) it. This indicates that there is a time period between the moment we pray and receive it spiritually to when it manifests physically, so that during this time we will have to walk by what we believe, in faith, and not by what we see. We are to believe we have received it before we see it manifested.

We are then expected to continue to believe we have received the answer before we see it. You may ask: How can I believe I have my healing without seeing it? That is what faith is all about! If we could see or feel it, then we would not need faith.

Now we know that when we ask God for healing according to Mark 11:24, He must instantly give us healing in some form when we ask, so that we can believe we receive it when we pray. But we have seen that He does not give us a *manifestation*—but He may do this on other occasions when He initiates a healing by a gift of the Spirit.

HEALING POWER

So if this healing does not come in the form of a manifestation, in what form does God give us healing when we pray? We must know what He gives or we will have difficulty believing we receive it. We won't know what to receive and so we will be open to confusion.

If not healing manifestations, then what does God always give us when we pray or when we have hands laid upon us for healing? What can we confidently believe we receive from God when we ask for healing?

We will see that the clear answer given by the Bible is that: God gives us *healing power* when we pray, and He expects us to believe we receive it when we pray!

What God gives to those who need healing today is exactly what Jesus gave the sick in His ministry. Jesus and the Father are One (see John 10:30, 14:10, 5:43, 13:20, 5:19). Jesus came in His Father's name, as His perfect Representative, coming to do His will and showing us exactly what He is like and how He works. Jesus did the works of the Father. In fact He said that the Father in Him did the works. He is the perfect will of God in action. This means that the healing ministry of Jesus was just the same as if the One who sent Him was there Himself.

God never changes. He is the same, yesterday, today, and forever. God has not changed His way of healing the sick, so if we find out what He gave the sick through Jesus, we will also know what He gives the sick today. So what did Jesus give the sick when they came to Him for healing? He could only give them what He had. For example, I cannot give you an ocean liner, because I don't have one!

In His earthly ministry, Jesus did not independently operate in His inherent divine power to give instant manifestations, for He had laid aside His glory and powers as God, in order to operate as a man totally dependent upon His Father (see Phil. 2:7-8). Therefore, in His humanity He did not automatically possess healing power. He had nothing to give the sick before He was baptized at the age of 30. He did no healings until then. Why? He had nothing to give the sick.

So what did Jesus receive at His baptism that He did not have before that He could give to the sick? God gave Him an *anointing* of the *Holy Spirit:*

> *When all the people were baptized, it came to pass that Jesus also was baptized; and while He prayed, the heaven was opened. And the **Holy Spirit** descended in bodily form like a dove **upon** Him, and a voice came from heaven which said, "You are My beloved Son; in You I am well pleased* (Luke 3:21-22).

Jesus explained this later by saying, "The *Spirit* of the Lord is upon Me, because He has *anointed* Me…to *heal*…to *set at liberty* those who are oppressed" (Luke 4:18).

This *anointing* clearly included *healing power.* He now had something to give the sick—*healing power.*

Acts 10:38 says that Jesus generally healed the sick by giving them the healing power that God had given Him at His anointing:

> *God **anointed** Jesus of Nazareth with the **Holy Spirit** and with [heal- ing] **power**, who went about doing good [freely distributing this healing power that He now possessed in abundance] and **healing all** who were oppressed by the devil, for God was with Him.*

Clearly this anointing or power was healing power, because of the re- sults it produced, "He went about *healing all* who were sick!" Jesus now had something to give the sick.

Jesus either gave them:

1. *Manifestations of the Spirit,* but these were special cases where God initiated the healing, as the Spirit willed—gifts of healings as in First Corinthians 12:7-11, or

2. *Healing power.* This is what Jesus always gave to anyone who ini- tiated their healing, who came to Him for healing. Generally, Jesus gave healing power to the sick and it healed them.

Acts 10:38 reveals the three beliefs needed to believe we receive healing:

1. God's will is to heal all, for His healing power is available for all, and Jesus used it to heal all who were oppressed by sickness.

2. God is a liberal Giver of healing. Having been richly anointed by God with healing power, He went about "doing good and healing all" the sick. "Doing good" describes an rich man who has so much money, he has enough to give away to anyone who needs it. Being generous, he then goes around freely distributing his riches to everyone who requests help. Therefore Christ, being a rich possessor of God's healing power, went about giving it richly to all who were sick. In this, He was showing us what God is like—a rich Giver.

3. Jesus healed all the oppressed by giving them God's healing power, with which He had been anointed by God.

In this ministry, God was working with Jesus. He was in full agreement with God, doing God's perfect will, showing us what God was like—that God is our Healer, freely giving healing in abundance and showing us how God heals; He gives us His healing power.

Luke 5:17 says: "...the power of the Lord to heal [healing power] was present" Jesus brought *power to heal* on the scene to give them. It does not say, their instant manifestations of healing were present.

Luke 6:17-19 says: "...the whole multitude sought to touch Him, for [healing] power went out from Him and healed them all." Notice that Jesus normally healed the sick by giving them God's healing power (not instant manifestations), which was and is still able to heal all people from all kinds of diseases.

GOD'S GIFT TO YOU

So what does God give the sick today when we ask Him for healing? He gives us His *healing power* or *anointing*.

God gives us His blessings in spiritual form (see Eph. 1:3) to be received by faith. As we then speak and act in faith, believing that we have received these blessings, they will come into manifestation. The instant we pray for healing or hands are laid upon us in faith for healing, the healing power of God is administered to our bodies.

So healing power is what the sick will receive today when they obey Mark 11:24. We consistently see that what God gave to the sick in the ministry of Jesus was healing power and He has not changed. So what God gives the sick today is His healing power.

> *When she heard about Jesus, she came behind Him in the crowd and touched His garment. For she said, "If only I may touch His clothes, I shall be made well." Immediately the fountain of her blood was dried up, and she felt in her body that she was healed of the affliction. And Jesus, immediately knowing in Himself that* **power** *had gone out of Him, turned around in the crowd and said, "Who touched My clothes?"* (Mark 5:27-30).

The woman with the issue of blood came to receive *healing* from Jesus. What did she receive from Jesus? *Healing power* that flowed out of Him into her and healed her. She was healed by healing power that was freely given to her by Jesus when she came to receive it by faith. This was the very same healing power that Jesus was anointed with in Acts 10:37-38, when He was baptized by John in the Jordan River. She did not receive an instant manifestation. Before the healing was manifested, the healing power had to be first administered and received, and it then quickly produced the manifested healing.

Jesus came to show us what God is like and how He works. If, during the ministry of Jesus, this woman received healing power from God through Jesus when she came for healing, then we will also receive healing power today when we ask Him in faith for healing. God does not change. God still heals us by giving us healing power that flows through Jesus from His death and resurrection.

Like this woman who was in need of healing, any recipient of God's healing power today must release their faith and believe they receive it when they pray or when hands are laid on them or when they make contact with it in some other way. Then the healing power of God, like heavenly electricity, will flow into their bodies and start driving out all sickness, recovering the body from a sick or weakened condition.

God's healing power is something real and substantial. It is God's love applied to our bodies.

We are told in Luke 9:1-2 and Matthew 10:1,8 that Jesus imparted His anointing to His twelve disciples and told them to heal the sick in the very same way: "Freely you have received [healing power], freely give [healing power]." They were to freely give healing power to any sick who wanted it.

Then in Mark 16:18, Jesus says of all Church-Age believers: "They will lay hands on the sick and [then] they will recover." *Recovery* indicates that we should expect a healing *process*, through the reception of God's healing power—not necessarily an instant manifestation. Recovery from sickness begins when the power (God's medicine) is received. Mark 16:18 says it begins when believing hands are laid on the sick; of course we can also believe we receive healing power directly from God in prayer.

So at the very same time when hands are being laid upon us, healing power is being given, transmitted, to us through the hands, so that we can believe we receive it into our bodies. We must believe we receive it when hands are laid on us, for it is our faith that gives action to the healing power, causing it to flow into us. From that moment, we can be confident that we have received healing power and that our recovery is under way. Thus we should then thank God for our healing—whether we felt anything or not.

HEALING HANDS

Mark 16:18 describes God's standard method of healing and says that God's healing power must first be administered and received through the laying on of hands and then this healing power will cause the manifestation of healing. So when we come to God and ask for healing, what God instantly gives us is His healing power, which we are to believe we receive when we pray according to Mark 11:24.

The story of Elizabeth, a member of my church, illustrates that it is healing power that God releases to us when we ask for healing. Elizabeth fell ill on May 10, 2010, and over the next few months was admitted three times to hospital. She was immobilized with excruciating pain in her legs. The doctors did everything they could, but they told her that it was beyond their knowledge.

On September 6, her friend Deborah, who was caring for her, told her there was a healing service at the church. Elizabeth wanted to attend and, with help, she struggled into the church on her crutches. When she was prayed for, she said she felt a power working in her legs, but she was not fully able to walk yet. Notice that this was not an instant manifestation, but God's healing power had instantly started to work. I told her to start thanking God that He was healing her, and to act on her faith by moving her legs as much as possible.

After a few minutes she was completely free! In her excitement, she held up her crutches for all to see and joyfully shouted how God had given her a miracle. She remains totally healed. Without the knowledge that it is healing power that God gives, we may not have been able to help her through to the full manifestation of her healing. If you think it has to be an instant manifestation, then even when you are aware of God's power at work, the fact the healing is incomplete may result in doubt entering your heart, causing you to turn your switch of faith off, so that God's power stops flowing and your healing fails to manifest.

Knowing that God gives us healing power when we pray enables us to believe we receive our healing when we pray; knowing the form in which it comes means that we can accurately receive it without confusion. Indeed, it is difficult to receive the healing power God gives if we are focused on experiencing an instant manifestation. It is impossible to believe we receive a manifestation. However, when we know that God immediately hears and answers us, by releasing the healing to us in the Spirit in spiritual form as healing power, then it is easy to believe we receive it.

When we know what God gives, our reaction after prayer will be so different. Before, we examined our bodies to see if God gave us an instant manifestation, and then got disappointed if nothing changed. But now when we have prayed and believed we have received His healing power, we will immediately thank God for this power that was administered to our bodies and confess that it is working in us. We are walking, acting, by faith in what we believe, not by what we see.

FEELINGS

We may be aware of the healing anointing and even fall down, but what really matters is receiving it by faith. One person may feel it and even fall, but not take hold of it. Another may feel nothing but take it by faith and get healed. If you feel it, take this as an extra confirmation—a sign of His presence to your senses—that God is giving healing to you, but don't depend on this feeling to know that the power is present and working. You must still trust the Word and believe you receive the power, for it is your *faith* that gives action to the *power* and allows it to accomplish its work in you.

If you feel nothing, you can still believe you receive, for true faith is based on the Word not on your feelings. If you feel the power, this can help stimulate you to believe you receive it, but your confidence must be rooted in the Word of God; for later on, in order to keep the healing power actively working in your body, you must be ready to stand your ground and maintain your position of believing that you received His power, and of believing and thanking God that this power is now working in you—even when you can't feel it.

If you just go by feelings, the moment you feel nothing, you will doubt and deny your healing, and the power you received will become dormant in you; *it is your **faith** that gives action to the power.*

HEALING TRUTHS

- The first three Steps we must take to be in position of being able to receive our healing when we pray is to know:

    1. God's *will* is to give *healing.*

    2. God's *nature* is to freely give *healing* upon request.

    3. God's *gift* to the sick is His *healing power,* flowing freely to us in the Spirit, on the basis of Christ's death and resurrection.

- God gives us healing power when we ask Him for healing and He expects us to believe we receive it when we pray! (See Mark 11:24.) However, we can't believe we receive an instant healing manifestation when we pray, because God never promised that.

- In the ministry of Jesus continued today in the Church:

    1. He sometimes initiated healings, as the Spirit willed, by being sensitive to the Spirit, but these were special cases. God still heals today through manifestations of the Spirit (see I Cor. 12:4-11).

    2. He generally healed by preaching the Word and healing all those who came to Him for healing—by their faith they initiated their healing. Jesus healed the sick by giving them God's healing power, which is still able to heal all people from all kinds of diseases.

- Jesus still heals the sick today by giving them His healing power. Although Jesus may give you a manifestation (gift) of healing, you cannot believe for this—it is only "as the Spirit wills." However, He will always freely give healing power to anyone who comes to Him asking for healing, which is well able to heal you.

Chapter Five

Know God's Method

STEP 4. KNOW GOD'S METHOD: LAYING ON OF HANDS

God gives healing power through the laying on of hands. Jesus said: "Therefore I say to you, whatever things you desire [such as healing], when you pray, *believe* that you *receive* them [healing], and you will have them [healing]" (Mark 11:24 KJV). This is a general prayer promise telling us how to receive the things that we need and desire from God, which include healing. These are the very things our loving, heavenly Father has provided for us in the New Covenant through the precious blood of Christ.

These spiritual blessings already belong to us in Christ (see Eph. 1:3), but we must still come to God, believing in His faithfulness to His promises and believe we receive them, according to Mark 11:24.

Thus in Mark 11:24, Jesus tells us to come to God in faith and believe we receive our healing. Often we have difficulty putting this into practice due to a lack of confidence before God, which comes from a lack of knowledge of His Word.

There are certain things we must believe in order to be in position to believe we receive our healing. We must know some truths about God before we can obey Mark 11:24. As each belief is formed and established in our hearts by the Word of God, we take another step toward the position of faith where we can believe we receive our healing when we pray.

We have previously discussed the first three key Steps:

Step 1: Know God's will: He wants to heal us. God is our Healer today. Healing and health is God's will for us.

Step 2: Know God's nature: He is a liberal Giver of healing. He answers us when we pray according to His will, His Covenant with us, giving to us liberally, richly, and freely, without delay.

Step 3: Know God's gift: He gives us healing power when we ask Him for healing—we must believe we receive healing power.

The steps that we have taken thus far to be correctly positioned and ready to believe we receive our healing when we pray are:

Goal Achieved: In a Position
to Believe to Receive
_____

Step IV. _____

Step III. Know God's Gift *(God gives healing power)*

Step II. Know God's Nature *(God gives without delay)*

Step I. Know God's Will *(Healing is God's will for me)*

You now know: (1) what His will is, (2) what He is like, and (3) what He gives.

You now know: (1) that healing is God's will, (2) that He freely gives us healing immediately upon request; He will not withhold it from us, and (3) that what He gives us when we pray is healing power.

It is healing power that God gives us when we come to Him for healing, and so it is healing power that we must believe we receive from Him when we pray.

Now we come to the final Step we need to take—the final belief that needs to be established in our heart from God's Word—in order to be in position to believe we receive our healing with confidence.

This final Step is knowing the answer to the Question: *How* does God give healing power to us? In other words: What is His method of delivery? To be in position to believe we receive our healing when we pray, we must also know God's method through which He gives us healing.

Step 4 answers: How does God give healing power to those in need of healing?

Answer: God gives healing power to the sick through hands.

Actually there are a number of different methods by which God imparts healing to our bodies, but the primary method is the laying on of hands. Please take time now to read the important information in Appendix A— God's Methods of Healing.

Jesus believed so much in the method of laying hands on the sick in order to minister God's healing power to them, that He used it as His primary method of ministering healing (see Appendix A). Moreover, He told the Church to continue His ministry of healing (see Mark 16:15-18), telling us all to continue to use the laying on of hands as the main method of healing. He said, "...He who believes in Me, the works that I do he will do also..." (John 14:12). These works include healing through the laying on of hands.

Jesus commissioned the Church to use this method to heal the sick, in confirmation of the Gospel we share:

> *"Go into all the world and* **preach the gospel** *to every creature. ...And these* **signs** *will follow those who believe:* **in My name...they will lay their hands** *on the* **sick** *and they will* **recover.***" So then, after the Lord had spoken to them, He was received up into Heaven, and sat down at the right hand of God* (Mark 16:15-19).

Then after the ascended Lord poured out the Holy Spirit upon the Church:

> *They went out and preached* [the Word] *everywhere, the Lord* [by His Spirit] *working with them* [the Word] *and confirming the* **word** [of the Gospel] *through the accompanying* **signs** [healings] (Mark 16:20).

This shows the laying on of hands is God's ordained method for the transmission of His healing power to the sick to cause their recovery. This Commission is for all believers in the Church Age. Therefore the laying on of hands is something that all believers are authorized to do, showing that it is God's general method to minister healing, rather than some special method for occasional use only.

PUTTING THIS METHOD INTO PRACTICE

This passage of Scripture in Mark also gives instruction on how to put the laying on of hands into practice. It connects the ministry of healing through hands with the preaching of the Gospel, the Good News of Christ.

We often see this connection in the ministry of Jesus Christ. First of all, He preached the Gospel. Then He healed the sick. See Matthew 4:23, 9:35, 11:5; Luke 6:17-19, 8:1-2, 9:11.

People came to *hear Him* preach the word of healing and then to be healed (see Luke 6:17).

Jesus then sent His disciples to preach the Gospel and then, heal the sick (see Matt. 10:7-8; Mark 6:12-13; Luke 9:2,6, 10:9).

Then He told the Church to preach the Gospel, and then lay hands on the sick and they will be healed (see Mark 16:15-18).

The first believers then obeyed by preaching the Word, and then seeing signs (healings) following the Word (see Mark 16:19-20).

In Mark 16:15-20, *healings* are described as *signs* or visible proofs that *follow* and *confirm* the *word* that is preached. So first of all the Gospel must be preached and then the healings will follow. They must receive the Word in order to be ready to receive the healing. So we must share the Word of God, before we minister healing. Then the result, their healing, will confirm the word they heard. This means the Gospel we share must include healing.

THE GOSPEL SUMMARIZED IN BELIEFS 1-4

The *Gospel* is the *Good News* summarized in Beliefs 1-4:

I. The Lord Jesus Christ is the Savior and Healer today. He wants to save and heal us.

2. Through Christ—His death, resurrection, ascension, and out-
    pouring of the Holy Spirit—God's power to save and heal is
    available now for all of us and will be freely given to us upon re-
    quest when we come to Him and call upon Him (see Rom.
    10:13).

3. When we ask Him for *salvation*, His *saving power* through the
    Spirit will come into our spirit to regenerate us, changing us
    from spiritual death to life. Likewise, when we ask Him for *heal-
    ing*, His *healing power* will come into our body to heal us, bring-
    ing us out of sickness and into health.

4. One way, ordained by God, that He gives or imparts this healing
    power to our bodies is through the laying on of hands, so that
    when hands are laid upon us, we will start to make a recovery.

Therefore we are to tell those in need of healing: "Christ died for your
sicknesses and sins, so He wants to heal you. On the basis of His death and
resurrection, He is ready to give healing to you, so that when hands are laid
upon you, God's healing power will be imparted to you. It will flow into
your body, and you will start to recover."

So their recovery will confirm each part of our message, we must share
with them this vital knowledge from the Word:

I. The Gospel makes God's power present to heal (see Rom. 1:16).
    For them to receive healing power, it must first be made present,
    and this is done by speaking the word of healing:

    > ...*they went out and preached* [the Word] *everywhere, the Lord*
    > [in healing power] *working with them* [the Word] *and con-
    > firming the word through the accompanying signs* [healings]
    > (Mark 16:19-20).

    The Lord's healing power works hand in hand with His Word,
    it accompanies the Word, it's made present through the Word.
    Unless we give the Word, the power will not be present for them
    to receive.

2. The Gospel, His Word, imparts the faith people need to receive healing power (see Rom. 10:17). If we don't share the Word they will not have the faith to receive His healing power. In order for them to be in position to believe they receive their healing upon the laying on of our hands, they need to have taken the four Steps, by attaining the four key beliefs from God's Word that we have been discussing.

Healing power must first be made present by the Holy Spirit and then it must be administered to the body by hands or the spoken word. The power can either be made present by the initiative of the Spirit, by a gift of healing as the Spirit wills, or by the initiative of the minister by sharing the Word of the Gospel. Therefore, unless the Spirit Himself is initiating the healing, before we use the laying on of hands, we must first share the Gospel, so that first and most importantly, God's power to heal is made present to them. And second, they have the faith to receive it when hands are laid on them.

The Word is God's conduit through which His power flows to us. When the Word of Christ is preached, the power is made present. When the Word of Christ is believed, the power will be received.

RECEIVE THE POWER

What is the Word we must share to make the power present? It is the Gospel of Christ, the Anointed One and His anointing. It is the Good News that: (1) Christ died for our diseases, to purchase (provide) healing for all of us; therefore healing is God's will for us, and (2) Christ died, rose again, ascended on high and received from the Father the Holy Spirit, whom He has now poured out upon us so the Spirit of the Lord (the anointing to heal) is now upon us for others.

The healing power of Christ is present now, for you to receive as a free gift from God. As I speak to you in the name of Jesus my Lord, the Kingdom of God—His healing power—is now at hand, it is here for you to reach out and receive. I am holding your healing in my hands. It is up to you now to take it. If you believe the Word that God's healing power is present here now for you, then receive it!

Notice the power is made present by the proclamation that "the power is present now," along with the explanation of how this is so. This is because the power of God is in His Word is in agreement with His Word, works with His Word, and confirms His Word.

So when you proclaim that, on the basis of Christ's death and resurrection "the power of Christ is present now to heal," you are making that power present to them through your very proclamation, "the *gospel* of Christ...*is* the *power* of God to salvation [healing], for everyone who believes" (Rom. 1:16).

This proclamation is exactly the message of *Jubilee* that on the basis of the atonement, God's grace and power to forgive and restore is here now for you to receive. It was the very proclamation of Jubilee, the blowing of the trumpet, that made the power present to the people so they could receive it. Until they heard the trumpet blast, they could not claim their freedom, for although it had been purchased by the atonement, it had not been made present to them—neither, of course, could they have the faith to receive it.

This is the same Gospel, the Good News, that Jesus preached. Though He preached before the cross, He still made the proclamation that the Spirit of the Lord, the anointing, was present upon Him to *heal*—upon the basis of His baptism, which was a Type of His coming death and resurrection. He declared that it was now the acceptable, or Jubilee, Year of the Lord, the time when people can come and receive, claim, God's grace and power that has been freely given to all (see Luke 4:18-21).

Jesus preached this message everywhere He went (see Acts 10:36-38), preaching the Good News that the Kingdom of God, His grace and healing power, was within reach for them to take hold of and receive. It is the very proclamation that "the power is at hand," that causes God's power to be at hand (present) to receive.

The Kingdom Is at Hand

John the Baptist was the first to make this proclamation, saying, "Repent, for the kingdom of heaven is at hand!" (Matt. 3:2).

Then "Jesus began to preach and to say, 'Repent, for the kingdom of heaven is at hand'" (Matt. 4:17).

Mark 1:14-15 says, "Jesus came to Galilee, preaching the gospel of the kingdom of God, and saying, 'The time is fulfilled, and the kingdom of God is at hand. Repent, and believe in the gospel.'"

Then, Jesus sent His disciples with the same message saying, "As you go, preach, saying, 'The kingdom of heaven is at hand'" (Matt. 10:7). The Kingdom of God includes every spiritual blessing, such as joy, righteousness, peace, and healing in the Holy Spirit: "the Kingdom of God is...righteousness and peace and joy in the Holy Spirit" (Rom. 14:17). So, when they proclaimed the Kingdom of God was at hand, they were declaring that God's healing power was at hand for them to reach out and receive.

In Matthew 11:12, Jesus explained what was happening: "From the days of John the Baptist until now the kingdom of heaven suffers violence, and the violent take it by force." An alternative way to translate this is, "The kingdom of heaven forces itself on men's attention, and forceful men lay hold of it."

This confident Gospel proclamation created a confident response, so that people laid hold of, claimed, their salvation and healing.

We are considering what is the Word that we should share to prepare people to receive healing through the laying on of hands. If we look from the viewpoint of what they need to believe in order to receive their healing, we have already discussed the four key beliefs, or Steps, they need to have to be in position to receive their healing. We saw that the truth contained in the first two Steps require us preaching the Gospel (Jubilee) message, and this is exactly what we need to share in order to make the power present to them! The final two Steps are specific instructions related to the special area of healing, so that they can believe they receive healing from God.

Thus before we lay hands on them, we should teach these beliefs:

I. God's *will* is to *heal* them, this is proved by the atonement.

2. God will *freely give* His healing to all who come to Him.

3. What God will freely give them is His *healing power*.

4. God will give healing power to them when our *hands* are *laid* on them, for this is a divinely ordained method of imparting healing.

In summary, we should tell people that God loves them and wants to heal them so much that Christ died to purchase healing for them. This healing is available and present now for them to receive. So the moment we lay our hands upon them, God will impart His healing power to their bodies and the recovery process will begin at once. We instruct them that when believing hands are laid upon them, they are to believe they receive their healing and then expect to recover.

We've seen that during His ministry, Jesus and His disciples used the laying on of hands as the main method of ministering healing to the sick. Moreover, we have seen that Jesus commissioned the Church to continue the ministry of healing using the same method.

We will now see from the Book of Acts that the early Church was obedient to do this and in so doing had great success. If we, too, are believing and obedient, we will also see success in the healing ministry!

In Acts 4:29-30 the Church prayed:

> *Now Lord...grant to Your servants that with all boldness they may **speak your word**, by **stretching out Your hand to heal**, and that **signs and wonders** may be **done** [come to pass, happen, made manifest] through the **name** of Your holy Servant Jesus.*

This prayer for success in ministering God's healing power reveals a lot about how it should be accomplished. The desired result is that healing is done by the power, Spirit, of God through the disciples as they speak and act in the name of Jesus. In the Bible, God's hand represents His Spirit of power; and when stretched forth, it represents the Spirit of God active, moving in creation, judgment, or salvation.

...He [Christ] *had rays* [of power] *flashing from His hand, for there His power was hidden* (Habakkuk 3:4).

...In Your hand is power and might; in Your hand it is to make great and to give strength [and health] *to all* (1 Chronicles 29:12).

Creation is the work of His hands and fingers (see Ps. 8:3,6, 102:25). Jesus identified the finger (hand) of God with the Spirit of God (compare Luke 11:20 and Matthew 12:28), saying that He cast out demons by the finger (or Spirit) of God. When He spoke a Word of command against a demon or a sickness, the Spirit of God went forth with the Word to remove it, compelling it to leave. The Spirit of God, the Father, flowed through His Son Jesus to heal the sick. Now He tells us to go in the place and in the name of Jesus and the Spirit of God's healing power will flow through us in exactly the same way.

The prayer in Acts 4 reveals that the Church knew that before *healing* the sick and seeing *miracles*, they must *speak* God's Word to them, for it is through God's Word that His power is made present. The Greek construction shows there are not two requests here (for *boldness* to speak, and for *healings*). Instead, their prayer was simply for God to enable them to fully speak His Word (Acts 4:29); they knew that whenever God's word of healing is spoken, His hand of power, the Holy Spirit, will be stretched out to heal (Acts 4:30):

...grant to Your servants that with all boldness they may **speak** *Your Word, by stretching out Your* **hand** *to* **heal***, and that* **signs** *and* **wonders** *may be done...* (Acts 4:29-30).

The clause "by stretching out Your hand to heal" is a temporal clause, indicating that this is happening at the same time as they are speaking the word. A clearer translation would be: "...grant to your servants that with all boldness they may speak Your word, while You stretch out Your hand to heal and that signs and wonders may be done..."

Whenever God's word goes forth, then the power of His Spirit is released (as in Gen. 1:1-3). "By the *word* of the Lord the heavens were made, and all the host of them by the *breath* [Spirit] of His mouth" (Ps. 33:6).

When God spoke His word, then His Spirit (Breath) also went forth to perform the word. His Spirit worked with the word to bring it to pass.

Likewise, because God has authorized us to speak His word in His name, whenever we speak the word of healing, the Lord, by His Spirit, will be working with the word we speak (see Mark 16:20), making the power to heal present (see Luke 5:17).

We see God's hand of working with His word in Acts 11:20-21, "...*Preaching* the Lord Jesus. And the *hand* of the Lord was with them, and a great number believed and turned to the Lord." Luke 5:17 says, "...as He was teaching [the word of healing], ...the power [hand] of the Lord was present to heal them [all]." And Mark 16:20 says, "They went out and preached [the word] everywhere, the Lord [by His Spirit] working with them [the word] and confirming the *word* through the accompanying signs."

THE PRESENT HEALING POWER

As we share the word, God stretches out His hand to the sick person to provide healing. God is holding abundant healing power in His hand. He is reaching out with an open hand to the sick, offering His healing power as a free gift. By the preaching of the word, His power is brought close to them, so that healing is at hand for them, so they can reach out and take it with their hand of faith. It is now up to them to believe the word and come to God and believe they receive His healing.

What is the Word of Healing that must be preached with boldness? We must proclaim that healing is at hand, to be received as a free gift; that God's hand is stretched out to heal them. As we declare it, then so it is (see Rom. 1:16), for "no word of God is without the power to bring itself to pass" (Luke 1:37, a literal translation). Thus we are co-workers with God. We see what He wants to do, to stretch forth His Hand for healing, and speak it forth in His name, as present reality. As we do, He fulfills the spoken word and does it—He stretches forth His Hand to heal.

Once this healing power has been made present by the word, then it still needs to be received by faith. Once *God's hand of grace* is stretched out to heal, a *person's hand of faith* must still reach out and take hold of the *healing in God's hand.* This can be done by the person coming directly to God and believing he receives his healing. More often, however, people find it easier to receive God's healing power through the ministry of another believer. Therefore, once God's healing power has been made present, it must be ministered (in the name of Jesus) to the body of the sick person, usually through the laying on of hands, who needs to receive it by faith.

The disciples who prayed this prayer in Acts 4:29-30 understood this, for they said that when they preach the word of healing, God's hand will be outstretched, "to heal, and that signs and wonders may be *done* [by believers] through the name of...Jesus." It is clear that unless God's *healing hand* is outstretched, there can be no healing. But notice that even when God's hand is outstretched for healing, something else needs to take place before healings happen. Even when healing power is present, *healing* must still be *done* through the name of Jesus.

This reference to the name of Jesus proves that healing is to be done by believers using His name—believers, not God, do things in the name of Jesus, as His representatives. The *power to heal* is present, but believers must take this power and deliver it to the sick. They are to take God's hand of power and apply it to the sick. The healing in God's hand must be given, ministered, to them and received by them. This is normally to be done through the laying on of hands in the name of Jesus (see Mark 16:18).

Thus the Church needed boldness to both: (1) *speak* the word of healing to make God's healing power present, and (2) *do* or perform the healings by administering healing power to the sick in the name of Jesus. However, it seems that they mainly prayed for divine boldness or confidence to speak the word of healing, for they knew that everything would follow from that. You see, they would have the confidence to lay their hands on the sick and heal them, if they knew that God's healing power was present. But they knew that it would be present if they were enabled to speak the word of God with boldness. Therefore, they simply needed to ask God to empower and embolden them to speak the word of healing as they should, knowing that then His power to heal would be present; which in turn, would give them the confidence to minister it to the sick.

TWO-STAGE PROCESS FOR MINISTERING HEALING

Acts 4:29-30 reveals a two-stage process for ministering healing:

"Lord…grant to Your servants that with all boldness they may (1) *speak Your word*, while You stretch out Your *hand* to *heal*, and that (2) signs and wonders may be done [by us] through the *name* of Your holy Servant Jesus."

When we *speak the word*, God *stretches* out His *hand to heal*, His power is then made present. Then this *healing power* must be given, administered, to the sick in the *name* of Jesus, which they must receive. The result is that the hand of the Lord, the Spirit, will manifest and accomplish His healing in them.

When the power (hand) of God is involved in creation or judgment, then only the first stage applies, for God speaks His word and it is done, performed. But when we are talking about the power of God unto salvation and healing, then both stages are required because of free will. Not only must God's word be spoken, bringing His power to people and making it present and active, but it must also be received:

The Gospel (Word) of Christ is the power of God unto salvation (healing), (2) for everyone who believes (see Rom. 1:16). Here we see that the Gospel when preached brings God's saving and healing power to people. His Spirit of power goes forth with His word, but it is only effectual for those who believe and receive.

Isaiah 65:1-2 predicts the salvation of the Gentiles through the Gospel:

> …*I was found by those who did not seek Me. I said, "Here I am, here I am"* [this is the preaching of the Gospel: the power of God is here to save you] *to a nation that was not called by My name. I have stretched out My hands all day long to a rebellious people* [Israel]. …

This prediction is quoted in Romans 10:20-21 in the context of the preaching of the Gospel, to show how the differing responses of the Gentiles and the Jews to the Gospel was prophesied. Notice how God is reaching out to all people through the Gospel, saying, *"Here I am"*; and as this message is spoken, He is stretching out His hands to us to save us, heal us, and receive us.

However, not all receive His offer. Some remain rebellious and reject Him, and so they do not receive the benefit of the outstretched hand, the Spirit, bringing salvation. Isaiah 53:1 tells us that the one to whom the arm (power) of the Lord is revealed is the one who believes the report (see Isa. 53).

The prayer of Acts 4:29-30 for boldness to preach the Word and to do healing in Jesus' name is based upon Mark 16:15-18, where Jesus told us to: (1) Preach the Word, and then (2) Lay our hands on the sick, in His name, with the promise that God's power would then surely flow into the sick and cause them to recover. This proved that the laying on of hands is a God-ordained method of healing, for He promises to always work with it by releasing His healing power to the sick causing them to recover.

Thus the working of God's healing power depended entirely on the disciples' obedience to preach the Word, and then to lay their hands on the sick, for God was ready to do His part and work with them to confirm His Word. Therefore, they prayed for all boldness, courage to do this. They knew that they needed God's help to speak the Word with freedom and conviction, without compromise or dilution, especially as they faced opposition. Knowing that the more confident and accurate we are in speaking the Word, the greater degree of power is made present to the hearers. And the greater degree of faith to receive is produced in the hearers leading to doubly greater results—we also need to pray for His ability to speak it fearlessly and fully.

Mark 16:20 then describes the two results of obedience: (1) When they preached the Word, the power of God was present and working with the Word. By speaking the Word, they activated the power of God that was upon them. Then (2) when they laid their hands on the sick in His name, the power of God visibly confirmed the Word by going into their bodies and working a complete healing.

In computer language, when we preach the Gospel we bring the power of God "online" for people, for them to download, receive. In the case of healing, the normal way for them to receive, having heard the Word, is through the laying on of hands in Jesus' name.

As mentioned previously, imagery of the prayer in Acts 4:29-30 confirms this use of hands to minister healing to the sick: "Lord,...grant...that with all boldness they may speak Your word, while You stretch out Your hand to heal, and that signs and wonders may be done [by us] through the name of...Jesus."

1. They see the Lord stretching out His hand toward the sick in healing power as they preach His Word. This is surely based on seeing Christ do this literally on thousands of occasions, for this was His normal way of giving healing to the sick.

2. They know that it is not enough for God's outstretched hand of power to be present, but that they must also apply it to the sick in the name of Jesus. They are not just to speak in His name, but also act, perform healing, in His name. See John 14:12 and Acts 2:43 says, "many wonders and signs were done [performed] through the *apostles* [as they ministered in His name]" (see also Acts 3:6,16; 4:10).

HOW TO DO THIS?

They knew they were to heal the sick in His name. But how were they to do this?

To speak and act in His name is to take His place and represent Him on earth with His authority, and say and do on earth what He is saying and doing in Heaven—just as Jesus ministered in His Father's name, saying what He heard the Father saying, and doing what He saw the Father doing. When we truly do this, He works with us and His power flows through us, accomplishing great things, confirming the Word, just as Jesus said that the Father in Him did the works.

So in taking the place of Jesus, we are to preach what He preached, the Gospel of healing, and do what He did, lay hands on the sick to give them His healing power. Moreover, we are to say what He is saying now, and do what He is doing now in Heaven. He is speaking His Word of grace, so that when we speak this same word on earth, His power goes forth, His hand is stretched out to heal the sick. Then, as we do on earth what He is doing in Heaven, and stretch out our hand in His name to heal the sick,

His power will surely flow through our hands into their bodies! As we speak His words in His name, He speaks through our lips. As we lay our hands upon the sick, He lays His hand, Spirit of healing power, upon them. As we speak and act in His name, He speaks and acts through us. As we preach His Word and stretch out our hands in His name, it is just as if Jesus Himself was personally laying His hands on the sick, so we can be sure that His power will flow through us to heal them! As He once healed through His hands, so He now heals through our hands.

Acts 4:29-30 paints a dynamic picture of how God and humankind work together in healing ministry. It reveals that when we speak the word that God has told us to speak, which includes declaring that God is now stretching out His hand to heal them, then God fulfills this word by stretching out His hand for healing, causing His healing power to be present. When we also do what He is doing and stretch out our hands to heal them in His name, obeying what He has told us to do with this power, then healing will be accomplished in them. The moment we lay our hands on the sick, He lays His hand upon them—His power flows into them. It is as if our hands become one with His hands!

This is all the more appropriate when we consider that we are now the Body of Christ; we are His feet, mouth, and hands on earth, to go to the sick, speak His word to them, and lay hands on them. Our lips are His lips for Him to speak through, our hands are His hands for Him to reach out with and touch the sick. So when we lay our hands on the sick in His name, it is His hands touching them. Therefore the Spirit will flow through our hands, as if Jesus Himself were there in the flesh touching them, for we are identified with Him.

In Acts 4:31,33 and 5:12 we see how God answered the prayer:

> ...*they were all filled with the* **Holy Spirit,** *and they* **spoke the word of God** *with* **boldness.** *And with great* [healing] **power** *the apostles gave* **witness** *to the resurrection of the Lord Jesus. And great grace* [anointing] *was upon them all. And through the* **hands** *of the apostles many* **signs** *and* **wonders** [miraculous healings] *were done among the people....*

They received boldness to *speak* the Word as witnesses—those who give testimony and evidence—that Jesus had conquered death. This Word caused God's power to be present, so that with this power they could do miraculous healings in Jesus' name, and so provide supernatural proof confirming their message that Jesus was alive forevermore, having defeated sickness and death.

How did they use God's power to perform these healings for people? How were these healings done by the apostles? It was *through their hands* that God's *healing power* was imparted to the sick; and this *power* produced the *proof*, the manifested healings. Notice again that God's power worked through the laying on of hands:

> *They stayed there a long time, **speaking** boldly in the Lord, who was bearing witness to the **word** of His **grace**, granting **signs** and **wonders** to be done **by** their **hands*** (Acts 14:3).

Again, we see the disciples first of all preaching the Word (Gospel) of His grace: that salvation and healing was bought and paid for by the blood of Jesus, so that God's power to save and heal is present now, being offered to all as a free gift, to be received by faith alone. As they preached this Word, the Lord was moving to confirm and bear witness to it. It was the preaching of His Word, that brought His power onto the scene, for the Lord, as always, was working with His Word.

When the Word was preached, the Lord moved to confirm it by healing the sick, but He did not heal them directly, for it was granted to His disciples to heal the sick in His name. He granted the performing of these healings to the believers, by giving them His healing power (see Acts 1:8), and then by making it present and active upon them when they spoke His Word.

How then did they do the healings? *By laying their hands on the sick!* It was by their hands that the power of the Lord, having been made present by the Word, was given to the sick, causing signs and wonders—manifest healings. In this way, the Lord bore witness to His Word of grace. Again we see the believers used the laying on of hands to minister healing power to the sick, for this is an ordained method of God. He was again faithful to His promise to always work with this method (see Mark 16:18), for He granted healings to be done by their hands. He did this by giving them active healing power, for them to deliver by hand to the sick. He works the same way today!

> **God worked** unusual miracles **by the hands** of Paul, so that even handkerchiefs or aprons were brought from his body to the sick, and the diseases left them and the evil spirits went out of them (Acts 19:11-12).

These healings and deliverances were done by God's power, but how did God get His healing power to the sick? By Paul's hands! The healing anointing on Paul flowed through his hands into their bodies driving out all diseases and demons. Here we see that some, but not all, sickness is caused by demons, but that God's anointing, transmitted through touch—hands—is well able to drive out all demons as well as diseases, even without them being commanded to leave, which is the normal method of deliverance. The many deliverances happening in Paul's absence, with no command, through cloths containing this anointing being laid on the sick, confirms this.

> The father of Publius lay sick of a fever and dysentery. Paul went in to him and prayed, and he **laid** his **hands on him** and **healed** him. So when this was done, the rest of those on the island who had diseases also came and were healed (Acts 28:8-9).

Paul "laid his hands on him and healed him." Notice it was Paul who healed him by the transmission of healing power into his body through his hands. When they heard about God's healing power working through Paul's hands, they believed he was anointed to heal, and so came to receive healing power by the same method—the laying on of hands, which God honored, as always.

The laying on of hands is practiced throughout the Bible. The Jews believed in it (see Lev. 16:21:22). Fathers laid their hands on their children and pronounced blessings on them (see Gen. 48:13-20). They clearly believed in the laying on of hands for the purpose of transmitting blessing. That is why they often brought their children to Jesus, for Him to lay His hands on them and bless them; and He complied, showing that He believed in, endorsed, and practiced this. The laying on of hands was the main method Jesus used to administer healing power to the sick. Often people came to Jesus and asked Him to lay His hands on the sick, showing that they believed that something was given through hands. What was given? Healing power.

Jesus believed so much in this method that He commissioned every believer to use this method, promising us that healing power will be administered to the sick as soon as hands are laid on them, causing them to recover, "They will lay hands on the sick, and they [the sick] will recover" (Mark 16:18). The recovery process begins when healing power is administered through hands. Recovery cannot happen until healing power is administered. This verse in Mark tells us healing power is always given as soon as hands are laid upon us. The instant hands are laid on us, we should consider ourselves to be recovering because healing power is now in us and working mightily. If the sick would embrace this truth, it would eliminate much fear concerning whether they will recover or not.

Most people receive healing power more easily through the laying on of hands. This is because they are able to comprehend better that healing power is given after hands are laid upon them, rather than through the use of other methods. It is easier for them to believe that healing power is given to them when hands are laid on them, than when someone says to them "be healed" or when they simply ask for it in prayer. When Jesus had only limited success in Nazareth because of their unbelief, He was still able to heal a few sickly folk, but only by laying His hands on them (see Mark 6:5). It would appear that when no other method of communicating healing power was accepted, some still received through allowing Him to lay hands on them. It seems that this method will work when nothing else will.

The laying on of hands is the main way for most to receive the healing anointing. Hebrews 5:12-6:2 tells us that the laying on of hands is one of the fundamental doctrines of Christ, the Anointed One and His anointing, and is referred to as the milk of the Word. It is not a side issue, but a central doctrine of the Christian life to be believed and considered as normal Christian practice.

Milk refers to areas that young Christians should be taught, for it is the milk that they are most easily able to receive and benefit from. I believe it is easier for them to comprehend that healing power is given to their bodies after hands are laid upon them, than through any other method.

We have now completed our study of the four beliefs needed to put Mark 11:24 into practice to receive our healing. As we become fully persuaded of each belief in turn, we take the next Step toward the position of being able to believe we receive our healing when we pray.

Step 1. Healing is God's will.

Step 2. God freely gives us healing without delay.

Step 3. God freely gives us healing power.

Step 4: God will always give us healing power when hands are laid upon us for healing.

Once these beliefs have been formed in us by God's Word, it is worth defending them when doubts come to our mind. We do this by declaring out loud our beliefs and the Scriptures that undergird them.

We have now taken the four Steps to be in position and to be ready to believe we receive our healing when we pray.

> Goal Achieved: In a Position
> to Believe to Receive
>
> Step IV. Know God's Method *(God gives through hands)*
>
> Step III. Know God's Gift *(God gives healing power)*
>
> Step II. Know God's Nature *(God gives without delay)*
>
> Step I. Know God's Will *(Healing is God's will for me)*

It will become easy to obey God's instruction to believe we receive our healing when we pray, when the proper firm foundation of the knowledge of God has been built in our hearts from His Word.

ARE YOU IN POSITION?

Are you in position yet to believe you receive your healing? Honestly examine where you are in relation to your healing. Ask yourself: *Am I in the realm of having believed I received my healing, or am I still trying to get God to heal me?*

If you have not yet believed you have received your healing, ask: *Am I now in position to believe I receive my healing, or have I allowed thoughts to lead me away from the beliefs I must have?*

If you are not in position yet, ask yourself: *Which of the four beliefs am I not yet fully persuaded of? Do I believe that my healing is God's will? Do I believe that He will freely give me healing power upon request, or when hands are laid upon me?*

If your faith is weak in one of these areas, then study the relevant Scriptures.

You should now be in position to believe you receive your healing when you pray or when hands are laid upon you in Jesus' name. Having prayed, you will then be able to confidently proclaim that you now possess the answer, the healing power from God, because you have believed you received it based on the foundation of what you know from God's Word about God's will, nature, gift, and method. His will is healing. His nature is to give it freely. His gift is healing power. His main method is the laying on of hands.

By taking these four Steps, you should have now attained the position of being ready to believe you receive your healing when you pray, according to Mark 11:24. You have now completed Phase I.

HEALING TRUTHS

- The four Steps we must take to be in position of being able to receive our healing when we pray is to know:

    1. God's *will* is to give *healing*.

    2. God's *nature* is to freely give *healing* upon request.

    3. God's *gift* to the sick is His *healing power*.

    4. God's primary *method* of healing the sick is to give them His healing power through the laying on of hands.

- God's methods of healing include:

    1. The spoken word (of command).

    2. The prayer of faith.

    3. Touch, whereby healing power is transmitted through physical contact. This contact is usually established by the *laying on of hands*, but it could also be established by the *hands* of the one needing healing, or through anointed *prayer cloths*. Another variation of the laying on of hands is the *anointing with oil*.

- Laying on of hands: Jesus believed so much in the laying on of hands that He used it as His main method of ministering healing power to the sick. In Mark 16:15-20 Jesus commissioned the Church to continue His ministry of healing by using this method to heal the sick. Since it is a divinely ordained method of healing, God has promised to always work through the laying on of hands.

Chapter Six

How to Believe You Receive

Jesus said in Mark 11:24, "Therefore I say unto you, whatever things you desire, when you pray, believe that you receive them, and you will have them" (KJV).

We have taken the four Steps of *faith*, comprising the *four beliefs* necessary to attain the position of being ready to believe we receive our healing when we pray. We have now completed Phase 1.

PHASE 2

Phase 2 is to *pray* the *prayer of faith* and *believe* we *receive* our *healing*. When we do this, we enter the realm of having believed we have received, and we will then possess His healing power in our body, which will be actively working to drive out all sickness, heal us, and restore us to full health.

Receive Forgiveness. Before coming to God to believe you receive your healing, you must make sure you are in fellowship with God, for your faith will not work in the dark. You must be in the light of God's presence to come to Him and believe you receive. Unconfessed sin paralyzes your hand of faith, which you need to use to receive your healing from God. If you need forgiveness for a sin, then ask for it now, for He promises to forgive and cleanse you (see 1 John 1:9). One of the main sins that will stop your faith from working is unforgiveness, for immediately after giving instructions in Mark 11:24 on how to receive from God by faith, Jesus adds the warning that unforgiveness will hinder you from receiving from God:

And whenever you stand praying, if you have anything against anyone, forgive him, that your Father in heaven may also forgive you your trespasses. But if you do not forgive, neither will your Father in heaven forgive your trespasses (Mark 11:25-26).

Confessing your sin to God and apologizing to the person, if necessary, is a small price to pay to enjoy God's healing. Forgiveness is often necessary, but it is not enough to be healed, for you must still come to God and believe you receive your healing.

Challenge: It is time to *pray* and *believe* you *receive* your *healing!* If the foundation of the four beliefs is established in your heart, you are now in position to believe you receive your healing. When you know that God's will is to heal you, that He will give you healing as soon as you ask for it or have hands laid upon you, and that what He will give you is healing power, then you are surely in position to believe you receive your healing when you pray.

It is now a simple matter to comply with the instruction of Mark 11:24 and come to God with confidence to believe you receive your healing. So:

Let us therefore come boldly to the throne of grace that we may obtain mercy and find grace to help in time of need.

We can come boldly because it is a throne of grace, for through Christ's sacrifice, God is to us now a God of grace, richly pouring out His healing mercy for us as a free gift. We are to come and obtain—believe we receive—it, so that we will go away from the throne in possession of His healing power.

Let us consider the woman with the issue of blood described in Mark 5:25-34, as our example of how to receive our healing from God by faith. This Bible story is included to show us clearly how God's healing power operates and how we can receive our healing.

What we know about her and what happened:

She was *hopeless* and her condition *desperate:* "Now a certain woman had a flow of blood for twelve years, and had suffered many things from many physicians. She had spent all that she had and was no better, but rather grew worse."

She *heard* the word of healing: "When she *heard* about Jesus..." Before she could receive her healing from Jesus, she had to first have a sufficient knowledge of Him by hearing His Word. Likewise, we have accumulated this knowledge from His Word, so that we too can believe we receive our healing.

She came to Jesus and received His healing power:

> ..she came behind Him in the crowd and touched His garment. For she said, "If only I may touch His clothes, I shall be made well." Immediately the fountain of her blood was dried up, and she felt in her body that she was healed of the affliction. And Jesus, immediately knowing in Himself that [healing] power had gone out of Him, turned around in the crowd and said, "Who touched My clothes?" But His disciples said to Him, "You see the multitude thronging You, and You say, 'Who touched Me?'" And He looked around to see her who had done this thing. But the woman, fearing and trembling, knowing what had happened to her, came and fell down before Him and told Him the whole truth. And He said to her, "Daughter, your faith has made you well. Go in peace, and be healed of your affliction" (Mark 5:27-34).

When Jesus said, "Who touched Me?" His disciples were surprised because there was a whole crowd of people touching Jesus. What was different about this woman that caused her to receive her healing while others failed to do so? It is clear from the story that the key was her faith, not the sovereignty of God—He is sovereign, but He has sovereignly decided to provide healing for all His people, for them to come and receive by faith.

Jesus said to her, "Your *faith* has made you well." Her touch was different because it was a touch of faith. The healing power on Jesus was equally available to all, but she was the only one who made a demand on this power by touching Him in faith. When her hand touched Him, her hand of faith took hold of, received, the power that was upon Him; and as a result, Jesus felt the power go out of Him, and she felt it go into her.

This woman who touched Jesus' garment is an example to us all of how to receive healing from God. The fact that she was no special case is clear from the story of how this healing happened, for she did not come and make a special request to Jesus for her healing. Instead, she came from behind, without His knowledge, and just took it from Him! Thus this healing did not have her name on it, and anyone could have done the same. She was successful, and Jesus commended her confident faith—an example for us to follow. He did not condemn her for stealing, for she was only coming to receive something that He had already given.

If you come and take $20 from me, I will be upset; but if I am going around holding out $20 bills and telling everyone I am giving them away as free gifts, then I would be pleased if you believed my word, acted on it, and reached out to take it from my hand. This is exactly what Jesus was doing, as He went around preaching that He was anointed with healing power and that healing was at hand for them all to come and receive.

Most people were waiting for something special to happen, but this woman just took Jesus at His word and came and took the healing power she needed, that He had said was upon Him as a free gift for anyone to receive. He only realized that she had done this after she had taken it from Him, and even then He did not know who it was who had taken it—although He was fully God, He had to operate as a man and put Himself under human limitations. Thus she did not even ask for His permission to take it, and the full approval of Jesus shows that she was not out of order in doing this.

The fact that she could righteously and successfully take healing from Him without His knowledge, proves that healing power had indeed been put "on-tap," made freely available and present for anyone to receive it in the same way. That she was no special case and that anyone could have received healing power as she did, is confirmed by what happened soon after when many people received healing power from Jesus in exactly the same way (see Mark 6:54-56; Luke 6:17-19).

HEALING POWER IS LIKE ELECTRICITY

God's healing power is invisible, but very real and powerful—like electricity. You can't see it, but when it flows, you can feel and see the results it produces. Electricity can be present in a room and nothing happen and your senses will not be aware of anything, for it is not flowing. However, you will still believe it is present if you believe in the reliability of the supplier. It is made present to a room by a voltage being communicated to it. The power is ready to flow when the right connection is made and a demand put upon it, giving action to the power. Thus, the power can be present, but it must still be received for it to flow, work.

When electricity is present in a room, anyone can receive the benefits of it. It does not work for some, and not for others. It works for all. It is just necessary to believe the power is present, plug into it, and put a demand on it. Thus anyone can put the plug into the socket, establishing a point of contact, and turn the switch on. As long as the switch is on, the power will flow producing the desired results.

That is exactly what this woman did who touched the hem of His garment. Knowing that the power was present upon Jesus, she plugged herself into it by establishing a physical contact with Him, and then turned on her switch of faith, putting a demand on that healing power, receiving its flow into her.

For power to be present there must be an ultimate Source (God), a Generator (Christ) that converts it into a useable form of power, and an activated Delivery System (the Holy Spirit). Thus healing power comes from God, flowing through Christ, in the Holy Spirit.

Christ's anointing at His baptism was the Generator for His earthly healing ministry, and this power was carried to people in the Spirit upon Him. When He preached the word of healing, He activated this power, making it present for people to receive. By His death, resurrection, ascension, and outpouring of the Spirit, He has established an eternal, never failing Generator of healing power. Moreover, by His blood, He has paid the full price for this power, the bill is paid in full, so that there will never be any shortage of healing power. It will never run out. There is sufficient heavenly healing power to heal every sickness.

This power now comes to us from God, through Christ, carried by the Holy Spirit. This power is activated, made present and receivable, when someone speaks the word of healing. Then it is up to us to plug into that power, establish a point of contact, and turn on the switch of faith—believe we receive that power into us.

Faith and Four Beliefs

Let us take a closer look at the woman's faith—the kind of faith that receives. We have seen that her faith was based upon the word that she had heard. What knowledge must she have she gained from the preaching of Jesus in order to receive her healing in the way that she did? Her actions prove that she knew that it was God's will for her to be healed, that there was healing power upon Jesus available for all, so that He would give it to her as soon as she came to Him to receive it. She knew that this healing power would be transmitted to her by touch, for she said, "If only I may touch His clothes, I shall be healed."

In other words the woman who touched Jesus' garment possessed the four necessary beliefs which came from the words of Jesus that He was the Christ, the Anointed One, and that the healing anointing of God was present upon Him and was "at hand" for anyone to come and receive, take, from Him. If we also have these beliefs established in our heart, then we are ready to take the same action that this woman took and receive the same results.

God's healing power is still upon Jesus for us to receive. We need to come to Him just as this woman did, and receive our healing.

So, *how* did this woman put her beliefs into practice, and *receive?*

There are four logical Steps, beliefs, she took in receiving her healing. If we follow these same steps, we will have the same success that she did. If we come to Jesus like this woman, we will receive like she did.

Step I: Say it. She *said* in her heart, *When I touch Him I shall be made whole* (see Mark 5:28). She decided on the time, place, and method of healing.

She set a point of contact by choosing how and when she would receive her healing. She determined in advance the method by which she would receive (touch), and the moment when she would release her faith and believe she received her healing—the moment she touched Him. Her physical touch of Jesus was the point of contact for her spiritual touch, the release of her faith, when she would receive her healing. Likewise, we must determine in advance our point of contact. We should either say, decide, in our hearts: *When hands are laid on me, I shall receive my healing*, or *When I pray, I will come to God and believe I receive my healing.*

We do not receive healing by accident; we must do it on purpose. If we decide to receive through hands, we should first hear the word of healing, usually spoken by the one praying for us, for it is by the word that the power is made present and our faith strengthened. If we decide to receive through our own direct prayer to God, then we should speak out loud the healing Scriptures for the same reason. Notice that she was also specific in her decision as to what she would receive. She did not say, "When I touch Him, I shall be blessed."

In our electrical analogy there are many different devices we can choose to use to receive many different benefits, blessings. It is up to us to determine what we receive from God—if you desire healing, be specific and make the decision that you will believe you receive healing when you make your point of contact.

Step 2: Do it. "She came behind Him in the crowd and *touched* His garment." Having set her point of contact, she followed through on her decision and *did it*—she *touched* Him. This was no simple matter. She was in a weakened condition, feeling her uncleanness (according to Jewish ceremonial law) and knowing that people would disapprove of her actions. Moreover, the jostling crowd around Jesus made it hard for her to reach Him. She had to overcome many thoughts telling her it was too hard, she could not do it, that she did not have the right to do it, and that she should delay for a better time to get to Jesus. But she had made a quality decision to come to Jesus, touch Him, and receive her healing. So with supreme effort and determination, she pressed through the crowd and *touched* Him. She resolved that nothing was going to stop her from reaching Jesus!

If she had not made the quality decision to *touch* Jesus, these factors working against her would have persuaded her to give up, so that she would have failed to *do* what she had to *do* to make contact with Jesus. As a result she would have failed to receive her healing.

In order to come to Jesus, we may have to overcome our own crowd of negative thoughts and reasonings that get in the way and try to stop us from getting close to Jesus. Don't let any obstacle, difficulty, or distraction hold you back. Having made a quality decision to come to Jesus, take determined action, press through the crowd, and make your point of contact. In our electrical analogy, this is the action of establishing a point of contact by putting the plug in the socket. Whatever you have decided, put it into practice, whether it is to have hands laid upon you or to come to God directly in personal prayer.

Step 3: Receive it. The suffering woman had not just decided to touch Jesus, but to *receive* her healing at the very moment she touched Him. She had determined in her heart, *When I touch Him I shall be made whole.* Thus the physical touch was her point of contact to release her faith in God's promise and receive her healing.

So at the very moment she made contact with Jesus, she believed she received her healing. She knew what she was doing. She did this all on purpose, according to the decision previously made. Her faith pleased God, for she came to Him believing He is the Healer now, and that He is a generous Giver of healing, a Rewarder of those who come to Him diligently—having diligently prepared their hearts in His Word to be ready to receive the answer when they pray.

Likewise, at the very moment you establish your point of contact with God's power, either when hands are laid upon you or when you come to God in prayer, believe that you receive your healing in the form of healing power. The woman released her faith at this moment—point of contact— and *received* her healing. In our electrical analogy, this corresponds to *turning on the switch* . This puts an immediate demand on the power that is already present and available, so this power immediately flows into the appliance and starts to work. Thus she *turned on her faith switch* and immediately God's healing power—heavenly electricity—flowed out of Jesus into her and quickly worked to produce a healing in her.

We need to *plug in, and switch on,* and then enjoy the benefits produced by God's healing power. At the same moment she touched Him with her physical hand and took hold of the hem of His garment, she also touched Him with her spiritual hand of faith and took hold of His promised healing power.

This was the difference between her and the rest of the crowd touching Jesus: she touched Him with the *touch of faith.* God is Spirit, and He gives healing in spiritual form to be received by our spirit, into our spirit, by spiritual means—faith.

Step 4: Tell it. Keep the faith switch turned on. "The woman knowing what had happened to her, came and *told* Him the whole truth." This woman in Mark 5 is our example of what to do after receiving. She gave her testimony, and in so doing she confessed that she had received her healing. Having received healing power by faith, we need to follow her example and start confessing and testifying to our healing, giving thanks to God for it. In our electrical analogy, this helps to keep our faith switch turned on, which keeps His healing power working in us.

The *faith switch* describes our believing. We turned it on when we believed we received healing power; and as a result; power began to flow. If we allow doubts to enter our hearts so that we stop believing this, then we turn the switch *off;* and as a result, the power will stop working—it will be present in us, but dormant. Keeping the switch turned on means to continue to believe that we have received healing power and that it is working in us to make us whole. This keeps His power active and fruitful in us as it works in our bodies to drive out all sickness and fully restore our health.

Thus, the key to manifesting and keeping our healing is keeping our switch *on.* This woman healed shows us that the way to do this is by *speaking* words of faith, testifying to others, and thanking God for our healing, confessing that we have received His healing power and that it is working in us.

When the woman had completed these four Steps of Faith, Jesus set her forth as an example of faith for us all to follow in receiving healing, saying,

1. Daughter, your *faith* (believing she received healing) has made you well (her faith was necessary to receive God's power).

2. Go in peace, and *be (remain) healed* of your affliction (sickness) (by continuing to walk in faith, believing she has received healing).

The first sentence looks back at what happened, while the second sentence gives instruction for the future. Jesus makes her responsible to keep her healing, to keep the power of God working in her. He tells her to walk in peace, fellowship with God, and to keep her faith switch turned on to maintain her faith that the healing power of God is at work in her. Thus like her, Jesus tells us to believe we receive our healing, and then to continue to believe we have received it.

In order to stand in this realm of faith—keeping our faith switch turned on—we need to confess our faith in the healing power of God, which includes giving our testimony to others and our thanks to God. This is one reason why Jesus turned around and asked, "Who touched Me?" He wanted her to declare her faith and testify and give thanks, so by this she would learn to maintain and walk in her healing. By bringing forth a confession of faith from her that she had received her healing, He completed the process of faith in her. Having received it, she needed to own, confess it as hers, and give thanks to God for it.

Another reason that Jesus singled her out of the crowd was to present her as a perfect example of receiving healing power by faith. Having commended her faith, shown in all of the four Steps described, He then instructed her to maintain her healing by continuing in this faith she had demonstrated. She was to continue believing she had received her healing from Jesus, and to continue testifying and giving thanks to God for it.

This action of Jesus in setting forth her faith as an example for all to follow was successful. Soon after, we see many people deliberately walking in her footsteps, receiving their healing from Jesus through the very same process of faith. This proves she was no special case, but an example to us all of how to receive from God:

> ...*immediately the people recognized Him, ran through that whole surrounding region, and began to carry about on beds those who were sick to*

wherever they heard He was. Wherever He entered, into villages, cities, or the country, they laid the sick in the marketplaces, and begged Him that **they might just touch the hem of His garment. And as many as touched Him were made well** (Mark 6:54-56).

Phase 2 also includes *receiving your healing* by praying the prayer of faith according to Mark 11:24: "Therefore I say unto you, whatever things you desire, *when you pray, believe that you receive them,* and you will have them" (KJV).

Let us apply this to healing: "Therefore I say unto you, *if you desire healing, when you pray, believe that you receive healing,* and you will have *healing.*"

If you have been diligent in reading and studying the Word of God to prepare your heart, you can come to God now and receive your healing. It is your decision as to whether or not you receive the Lord as your Healer.

Say, "Father God, I come to You now in the name of Jesus. I thank You that You love me and want me to be healed and that You freely and generously give healing power to all who ask You, for by His sacrificial death on the cross for me, Your Son, Jesus, has purchased my healing. Right now, according to Your Word, *I believe I receive my healing.*"

After you have prayed in faith, *say,* "Thank You, Lord, for healing me. I have received it, so I have it now. I thank You that Your healing power is now powerfully working in me, driving out all sickness, restoring my health, and making me whole! Lord Jesus, You are my Healer and You are healing me now."

HEALING TRUTHS

- Jesus Christ, in Mark 11:24, promised: "Whatever things you desire [such as healing], when you *pray, believe* that you *receive* them [your healing], and you will have them [your healing]" (KJV).

- When the four beliefs are established in your heart, you have the necessary foundation of faith in your heart to obey Mark 11:24.

- Remember, (1) you must *desire* healing, then (2) pray, coming to God and looking to Him as the Source and Giver of healing, and then (3) *believe* you *receive* healing power, and you will have healing.

Chapter Seven

What to Do After Praying

In Phase 1, we took the four Steps to reach the position of being ready to believe we receive our healing when we pray.

In Phase 2, we prayed the *prayer of faith* and *believed* we *received* our *healing* when we prayed.

Now we move into Phase 3—*after* the prayer of faith.

PHASE 3

God is a Spirit, and He communicates Spirit to spirit. He gives us His blessings, including healing, in spiritual form. Thus He gives us healing power when we ask for healing, and He gives it in the Spirit, to our spirit. So we must receive it by spiritual means, by faith. Faith is a quality of our inner self, our spirit, for we have a spirit of faith (see 2 Cor. 4:13), and believing is a function of our spirits, for we believe in the heart (spirit) and with the heart (see Rom. 10:9-10).

Thus, in prayer, our spirit comes to God who is Spirit, and we believe we receive spiritual healing power with our spirit, and so it flows into our spirit. Then just as a natural heart pumps the life blood to every part of the body, so our spiritual heart will pump the healing power to whatever part of the body needs it (see Prov. 4:20-23; John 7:38). It is like a clearing house that receives life from God and then distributes it to our soul and body. This is how we can believe we receive something in the spirit when we pray, before we see it come into manifestation.

A PROCESS

When you believe you receive them, you then have them in your spirit, but you do not have them yet in manifestation, for there is then a process which must take place, in which the answer comes forth from your spirit into manifestation in your body. However, there is a promise here, that what you have received in your spirit will come into manifestation openly, as part of the normal process of faith, unless we do something to abort this process, which is described in Mark 11:23, as we shall see. The length of time this will take depends on what we are believing for, as well as how much spiritual life is issuing forth from our spirits through our hearts. This last factor is determined by our faith, and how much it is working. This depends upon us living in fellowship with God (prayer), putting His Word first, and guarding our hearts from unbelief (see Prov. 4:20-23), and also on the words we speak.

The purpose of this chapter is to show how this process works in more detail and how we can cooperate with it, so that the desired manifestation will come forth and not be delayed. One analogy we discussed is electricity. We saw that *believing* we *receive* healing power is like plugging in an appliance to the socket and *turning on the switch*. Thus the faith switch, which is either on or off, describes whether or not we believe we receive. Once we have turned on the switch, we must *keep it turned on*, if we want to keep the power flowing to produce the desired results.

Likewise, when we received God's healing power, our faith switch was turned on, but we must keep the faith switch turned on in order to keep God's power active, working, and fruitful in us, for us to get the full benefit. Keeping our switch turned on means to keep *believing:* (1) healing power has been administered to us and (2) it is working now to recover our bodies from sickness. This kind of *faith gives action to the power.*

It is like boiling a kettle. There is a process of time during which power flows while the switch is on. Initially it may seem like nothing is happening and this might cause us to turn the switch off, and then of course nothing will ever happen! But if we keep the switch on, believing that the electricity is flowing, then the power will flow and soon the heat produced, manifested, by the power will be obvious. The time taken to complete the full process of boiling, the complete manifestation, depends on: (1) the amount of water that has to be boiled (the physical need), and (2) the amount of power flowing into the water (the strength of flow of healing power). The degree of power-flow depends on the degree of healing power ministered and the degree of faith that received this power and that continues to put a demand on, give action to, this power to cause the desired results.

If we turn the faith switch off, the power will become dormant—it is present, but is no longer active or fruitful. If we have unbelief, so that we turned the switch off and shut the power down, we need to repent and re-activate! When we turn the switch on, the power becomes active again. Refuse to quit just because results don't come instantly. When we turn on the heating, the room warms up gradually as a process, as long as we keep the switch turned on!

It helps to keep the healing power turned on by *talking* about the power of God, where it comes from, when we received it, and what it is doing in us, and *thanking* God for it. Say, *"Thank You, Lord, for the healing power of God that has been administered to my body and is working in me right now to drive out all sickness and produce a complete healing in me."* You will keep God's power working in you if you stay loyal to your belief that God's healing power was given and is at work in you, holding fast to your confession of this.

Another analogy is the growth of a seed. The Bible often uses the growth of a seed to show how spiritual things work (see the Parables in Mark 4). God's healing power is like a *seed* growing within us. First of all, a seed must be received, planted, underground, in the invisible realm. Likewise, God's healing power must first be received into our spirits.

At first the seed seems small and insignificant, but it is full of life and potential. It contains the power and ability to grow and rise above the surface producing a wonderful outward manifestation, visible to all, whether a great tree or beautiful plant. Likewise, God's healing power is able to produce a complete healing in our bodies. Indeed, this will happen, as long as it is given the right conditions to grow in, for the growth and manifestation of a seed is the normal course of nature, and this mirrors how the blessings of God's Kingdom work and come into manifestation (see Mark 4:26-29).

For best results, we need to keep the soil, our hearts, in good condition, for it is functioning faith in the heart that causes the power to work, and to keep giving the seed water and nutrients, stimulating its growth, and to keep protecting it by removing, dismissing doubts and unbelief. Thus we are to regularly *water* and *weed* the seed, by hearing the *Word* and speaking it over ourselves (see I Cor. 3:6; Mark 4:8-9). When you have received God's healing power, relax because the seed is now planted in you and it is alive and working in you—even if you can't see or feel it. As you water it, by thanking God and confessing that His power is at work in you, then you know it is gaining strength and growing as a result, just as you do when watering a plant. If the plant's growth has become dormant and it is wilting from neglect, then you know that as you water it again, it will begin growing again and recovering its strength, even if you don't see an instant change. Notice if healing power, the seed, is neglected, it does not disappear, it is still present, but becomes dormant, inactive, and unfruitful—but you can reactivate it by watering it with the Word.

The final results and the time taken to produce satisfactory fruit depend on the care taken in nurturing the seed. However, by the very nature of a seed, there is process of growth that takes *time* to complete. This period of time of growth between *seed time* (planting) and *harvest* (full manifestation) requires *patience* (endurance) on our part.

We need *patience* in the time period between receiving by faith and the manifestation. The Book of Hebrews has much to say about this, for it is written to those who have believed the promise, but are under pressure to give up (stop believing). It encourages them in patience to not quit, but endure.

Let us look at some important verses:

Hebrews 6:12: Do not become sluggish, but imitate those who through: (1) faith and (2) patience inherit the promises. This tells us we are not to become weary and stop believing, but rather be like those who (1) believed they received the promise, and (2) continued to believe until they received the manifestation.

Many get discouraged and abandon their prayer if nothing happens quickly, but patience, continuing to believe, will be rewarded. Notice that it requires both faith and patience to see the promise fulfilled. It requires both initial faith and continuing, abiding faith.

Hebrews 10:35-36: "Do not cast away your confidence, which has great reward. For you have need of endurance, so that after you have done the will of God, you may receive the promise." If we do not cast away our confident faith, we will get a great reward—the open manifestation of healing. We need to patiently continue in faith, so that after believing we receive our healing, we may receive the healing manifestation in our lives.

The writer of Hebrews tells them to not cast away their confidence. This means that they already have confidence (faith); thus they have already received the promise by faith, according to Mark 11:24. Now he tells them that it is also important they maintain their confidence (in God and His Word), rather than throwing it away. They need to patiently stand in faith and continue to believe they have received healing power, until the healing comes through, otherwise they will not receive the reward—the manifestation of healing. Notice that the fulfillment of the promise in us does not just depend on us having confidence, faith, at one time, but upon us patiently keeping that initial confidence in God, even when pressured to discard it.

Hebrews 10:37-39:

> *For yet a little while, and He who is coming will come and will not tarry* [be encouraged the manifestation will come soon]. *Now those justified* [by faith] *shall* [also] *live by faith* [those who receive by faith, shall also live, be sustained, and receive God's life by faith]. *But if anyone draws back* [into unbelief] *My soul has no pleasure in him* [when we continue to believe God, we give Him pleasure, but not otherwise]. *But we are not of those who draw back to perdition, but of those who believe to the saving of the soul.*

The effect of continuing in faith is not just seeing the answer, but the saving of our soul, the development of patience and Christian character.

Hebrews 3:14: "We have become partakers of Christ, if we hold the beginning of our confidence steadfast to the end." The beginning of our confidence (faith) is when we believed we received the promise. We will partake of Christ and His healing if we steadfastly continue in faith until the end—the final manifestation of healing.

Again we see the importance of both faith and patience, if we are to fully partake of Christ and His blessings. The beginning of our confidence is when we initially believed we received our healing. We must also steadfastly hold this confidence firm, that we have received healing power and that it is now working mightily in us, until the end when the healing is fully manifested.

WHAT IS THIS PATIENCE?

Is patience just passive waiting? No, it is an active spiritual force, it is endurance, it is holding our confidence steadfast, even under contradictory circumstances. Patience is the word *hupermeno*. *Meno* meaning to abide, *huper* meaning under. So it means to continue believing and speaking the promise, even while under opposing pressures, contradictory circumstances, that press us down, for there is a stronger power within us, patient endurance, sustaining our will.

One important aspect of our patient believing in this time is keeping a good *confession* of what God is doing, for our *faith* is primarily expressed through our *words*.

Let's further examine Hebrews about this truth:

Hebrews 3:1: "Holy brethren, partakers of the heavenly calling consider the Apostle and High Priest of our *confession* Christ Jesus." Our heavenly calling includes healing. We are called to healing. Thus we are partakers of healing from Heaven, which we are also to confess.

Confession means to say the same thing as. Thus confession means to say the same thing as God says. To confess God's Word is to agree with His Word, speak His Word as true in our lives, and line up our lives with His Word, for it is true. It is to declare God's promises over our lives as true and established. What becomes manifested in our lives is determined by our faith and confession. Notice that the present ministry of Jesus for us in Heaven is linked to our confession. He is the High Priest of our confession, for the Spirit of Christ is sent from Him to fulfill the covenant in us.

What we confess before God, He releases the Spirit to perform in us. Thus Christ Himself stands behind our confession of God's Word. Therefore when tempted by unbelief, we should *consider Him* who stands behind our confession—is He not able and willing?

Hebrews 4:14: "Seeing that we have a great High Priest who has passed through the heavens, Jesus the Son of God, let us hold fast our confession."

We need to patiently hold fast to our confession. Let us keep saying the same thing as God's Word without wavering, for God is faithful to His promises. *To hold fast* implies there is a pressure on us to take the Word from us, doubts from satan or natural unbelief from being in the world, facing contradictory circumstances. We must keep a clear vision in our hearts of Jesus bringing it to pass. The ground of our confidence is not the power of positive talking but Jesus who stands behind our confession, because He stands behind His Word to perform it (see Jer. 1:12). We must see Jesus as our Great High Priest who continually ministers and mediates to us the life and blessings of the New Covenant according to our confession of faith. Seeing Him enables us to patiently hold fast our confession.

Hebrews 10:23: "Let us *hold fast* the *confession* of our *hope* without wavering, for He who promised is faithful."

Hope describes something we don't see yet, but which we firmly believe will come to pass based on God's Word. It's not just a wish, but a confident expectancy of a future manifestation. Our hope is our inner vision of the sure fulfillment, manifestation, of what we have received by faith, but don't yet see with our eyes. Therefore, we are told to continue to confess the end result of what we have already received by faith, even though we don't yet see it. We are to declare: (1) that we have received healing power, (2) that it is working healing in us now, and (3) that it will bring forth a complete healing in us.

Our full confession of faith covers the past, present, and future. We are told to hold our confession fast and to not waver or doubt, for doubts and pressures come from what our eyes see and ears hear, to try and make us change what we say into denial. We must not doubt or differ with the Word, but instead continue to confess it. To sustain our faith under pressure, we must meditate on God, considering the character of the One who made the promise. Our faith can only be as strong as our confidence in the reliability of the One who promised us healing.

We now take a closer look at how to express our faith during this time, in order to bring the healing into manifestation and to protect our hearts from the hindrance of unbelief. The same principles of faith that apply to bringing our healing into manifestation also apply to keeping it, once it is manifested.

EXPRESSING OUR FAITH

Next are four ways we need to express our faith during this time:

1. Thanksgiving to God

"...let us continually offer the sacrifice of praise to God, that is, the fruit of our lips, *giving thanks* to His name" (Heb. 13:15). We can continually give thanks for our healing because we have believed we receive when we prayed. Once we know healing power has been administered, the first thing to do is to give thanks. It is only polite, once we realize something has been given to us, to give thanks to the Giver. This is the sign that shows if people have believed they received when they prayed, otherwise they check to see if anything is different.

Those who know God will look to Heaven and offer thanks as soon as hands are laid upon them, for they know that they have received healing power and that it is working in them mightily. They are walking by faith, not by sight. Faith gives thanks, rejoicing in the promise, as if it were already fulfilled, because we have it. We thank God that it is ours now. Thanksgiving not only honors God, but it helps keep the faith switch turned on so God's power is active and working to manifest our healing. It is also the best way to keep what we believe in the forefront of our minds, keeping any doubts at bay.

This helps us to remain loyal to these beliefs formed in us from God's Word. We should express our gratitude to God for the four essential beliefs and for His faithfulness to give us healing power when we prayed, and for it working mightily in us now to heal us.

Medicine. Healing is a process, so if you are on important medication, don't stop it without your doctor's permission. Remain under the care of your doctor. Take what he prescribes. As you do, confess that God's healing power was given to you and is working in you. As it continues to work in you, you will find you will need it less and less, until you won't need to take it anymore. Suddenly stopping your medication will not cause the healing power to work faster, for it is your faith that gives action to the power. By all means, speak your faith and put your faith into action and start to act in line with the fact that God's healing is working in you, doing what you could not do before, but don't do anything unwise or unnecessarily put your life at risk by refusing medication. Don't receive condemnation if you need to take natural medication, which God has put in the earth for our benefit. Sickness is an enemy, so fight it with every means—natural and spiritual—at your disposal. The natural and supernatural working together make a powerful force for God.

Receive any medicine with thanksgiving, just like you receive healing power, saying, *"I receive this into my body. It goes to work doing good and no harm, bringing healing to my body. I believe God's healing power is working along with this medicine to remove all sickness and make me well. Thank You, Lord, for healing me and making me healthy, strengthening my immunity to sickness. Jesus, You are my Healer."*

In 2001, my wife, Hilary, developed an intestinal problem. Three hours after eating, she had intense pains that could last up to 17 hours and nothing would relieve it. All she could do was eliminate the foods that caused the most pain, leaving her to eat boiled eggs, rice cakes, skinless potatoes, and canned sardines. Over 18 months she lost over 28 pounds. Even then she still experienced bouts of strength-draining pain, lasting for hours. She would pray and believe God for healing, but when the pain struck again after eating she'd say, "My faith has failed again, what's the matter with me?"

Then she heard a testimony of a lady bedridden with terminal stomach cancer. She could not keep any food down and was so weak she could not sit up in bed. After praying for her, the minister encouraged her to start thanking and praising God. At first she was so weak she could barely whisper, but as she persisted her voice became louder and louder until she was sitting up in bed shouting praise to God. Eventually she was so strong she got out of bed.

He encouraged her to start eating straightaway, but she said, "I can't keep anything down. Every time I eat it comes back up!" He told her when she was about to eat to say, "'When I eat, it stays down and nourishes my body.' Say this and even if you throw up immediately, just wipe your mouth and say. 'When I eat, it stays down and nourishes my body.'" She became perfectly whole.

This was a life-changing revelation for Hilary. Every time she ate she said, "When I eat this food, it nourishes my body and is digested without pain." At first the pain came four hours after eating, but she kept saying, "When I eat this food, it nourishes my body and is digested without pain." After only three weeks of faithfully making this confession, she realized she had no pain and had been eating foods that previously had given her so much pain. The power of God was released as she stood in faith and held fast her confession and thanksgiving to God.

2. Confessing, Calling, and Commanding

Confessing, calling, and commanding all describe similar actions of our tongues. When we *confess* the Word, we are declaring God's promises over our lives. We can also *call, command,* our healing forth from our spirits. We have seen that when we believed we received our healing, we received by faith it in spiritual form, in our spirits. Now it needs to be brought forth from the spirit into physical manifestation. How is this to be accomplished? The Bible reveals this in Genesis 1:1-3.

God had the universe conceived within His Spirit (Being), but only when He *commanded,* "Light be!" did it come forth from His Spirit into manifestation. We are like a woman who has received the seed and is pregnant with a growing baby. So we are to give thanks to God for giving it to us, and then we bring it to birth, visible manifestation, by speaking, calling it forth. Say, *"Healing, come forth."* God brought the universe to birth this way. It was conceived in His Spirit, and then it came forth when He said:, "Light be!" He *called* or *commanded* it to come forth into manifestation by speaking it forth by words of faith. Only then did it come into sight.

He did this by speaking, commanding, the desired end result, calling what was not as being, and thereby He called it into being, for every Word of God has the power, Spirit, within it, to bring itself to pass (see Luke 1:37). God's Spirit goes forth with His Word to perform it. He brought forth what was inside Him to the outside by His words. This is how God Himself works! When we do this, we are operating in the God-kind of faith, for we are made in His image, designed to operate in His way, with His kind of faith. This is why Jesus said, "have the faith of God" or better, "have the God-kind of faith" (see Mark 11:22). This is the faith that "calls [forth] those things which do not exist [visibly] as though they did" (Rom. 4:17). It calls them forth from the Spirit into the natural realm, as God did at creation. We are to call forth into our bodies the healing we already received in our spirits.

Many Bible translations say: "Have faith in God," which is good advice of course, but not actually what Mark 11:22 says. Once we have received the answer in our spirit (see Mark 11:24), we speak it out (see Mark 11:23), operating in the God-kind of faith (see Mark 11:22), confessing and calling forth the desired end result, calling [forth] those things that be not [manifest] into being. We can say, *"Healing, come forth into my body."* By our words, we bring things out of our spirits into our natural lives. We call forth the desired result *into being*, by calling it *as being*, and this releases God's Spirit to manifest it.

By our words, we bring things out of our spirit into the natural. It is by our words that we call and bring forth what we already have received in our spirit into manifestation. A good man out of the good treasure of his heart brings forth good things. How? Out of the abundance of the heart the mouth speaks (see Matt. 12:34-37).

When Jesus commanded Lazarus to *"come forth"* (see John 11:43), He had already believed He received his resurrection from God in prayer (see John 11:42). He called, commanded, life to come back into Lazarus' body, and He called him to come into the light for all to see. He spoke the desired end result. He commanded it to come forth. He spoke out by faith, what He had already received from God through faith. We can only speak the command of faith, calling something forth into manifestation, when

God has already given it to us in the spirit. We must also be consciously trusting Him to bring it to pass.

Romans 10:8-10 also tells us that faith works this way: "The *Word* is near you, it is in your *mouth* and in your *heart* [that is, the *word of faith* which we preach]: that if you *confess* with your *mouth* the Lord Jesus, and *believe* in your *heart* that God has raised Him from the dead, you will be saved [receive the manifestation of the Word]. For [1] with the *heart* one *believes* unto righteousness [first you believe you receive the promise of righteousness or healing] and [2] with the *mouth, confession* is made unto salvation [then, having believed you received it, by confessing your faith that you have it, you bring it forth from your spirit into manifestation]."

The word of faith, which contains and brings to us the blessing and healing of God, must be in our hearts and in our mouths, for it to be fulfilled in us (see Rom. 10:8). We must believe in our hearts and confess with our mouths that Jesus is the Lord our Healer. By means of the word of healing in our hearts, with our hearts we are able to believe we receive healing power into our spirits. Then, by means of the word of healing in our mouths, we are able to bring forth our healing from our spirits into our bodies, by confessing our healing with our mouths, calling it forth into physical manifestation. We must confess with our mouths what we believe in our hearts—that healing is ours, for Jesus is our Healer. Confession is made unto salvation, manifestation.

The spirit of faith is, "we also believe and therefore speak" (2 Cor. 4:13). As we breath in and out, so we believe, we receive, healing into our spirits and confess it by faith out of our spirits into our bodies.

Romans 10:11-13 then gives us the basis for our confession of faith: "For the Scripture says, 'Whoever believes on Him will not be put to shame.' For there is no distinction between Jew and Greek, for the same Lord over all is rich to all who call upon Him. For 'whoever calls on the Name of the Lord shall be saved.'"

When we call upon the Lord for salvation or healing, He always gives it to us richly, so if we call upon Him for healing, believing we receive it, we shall surely have it in our spirit.

Therefore, we can rightly confess that healing is ours, calling ourselves healed—even if we do not yet see it—and as we do this, healing will be fulfilled in us. These verses in Romans promise that this process of faith will work every time, for God is faithful. Mark 11:23-24 also gives us this same guarantee.

The classic illustration of this two-stage process of faith is reflected in the life of Abraham and the key verse is Romans 4:17:

> (*as it is written,* [faith is based on the Word] *"I have made you a father of many nations"*) *in the presence of Him* [before Him] *whom he believed—God, who* [1] ***gives life*** *to the dead* [He is the Source of Life to those who know they need Him], *and* [2] ***calls*** [forth] *those things which do not exist* [be not] *as though they did.*

God works by (1) *giving* us *life*, which we are to *receive* by faith. Then (2) He *calls* it accomplished, and we are to agree with Him and *call* it done. In this way we call it into manifestation.

Abraham's Faith

God *called* the universe into existence by His words, but first He had to have believed-conceived it into His heart. In the faith of Abraham (see Rom. 4:17-21), we see the same two stages. As our father of faith, Abraham gives us the example of how to walk in faith, so we may "also walk in the steps of the faith" of our father Abraham (v.12), for the promises of God are for those "of the faith of Abraham, the father of us all" (v.16). His faith was based on God's Word (v.17). God gave him the promise that he was father of many nations, confirming this by changing his name from Abram to AbraHam (see Gen. 17:2-5).

This came to pass through his faith. We are to receive from God in the same way, so it is important to learn how his faith worked.

The first thing we are told about Abraham's faith in the promise is that it operated before Him or in the presence of Him whom he believed—even God, who (1) gives life to the dead and (2) calls those things which be not, as being, and so calls them into being (see Rom. 4:17).

This phrase carries much meaning. First, it says that he walked before God, in fellowship with God, for faith only works in the light of God's presence, our faith is personally trusting in God. It also describes a man in harmony with God, walking and working with Him, imitating Him. Seeing what He is saying and doing, he speaks and acts in line with that—as in dancing, following His lead.

This is what God told Abraham when He gave him the promise: "When Abram was 99 years old, the Lord appeared to Abram and said to him, 'I am Almighty God *walk before Me'*" (Genesis 17:1).

In this connection, we are told two things about God:

1. He gives life to the dead, and that is exactly what He was doing for Abraham and Sarah, who were as good as dead as far as re-production was concerned. Note: God gave *life* to Abram by giving him His promise: "You shall now be called AbraHam." So walking *before* God, they first had to believe in God as the *Giver* of life. They believed they received God's life into them according to His promise (see Mark 11:24). The adding of the "H" in the middle of his name (the sound of breath), signified the breath, spirit, life of God, which went inside him changing him from Abram to AbraHam when he received it. Likewise, Sarai received His life into her and became SaraH.

2. He calls into being (manifestation) those things which do not (yet) exist (in the natural realm), by speaking the word of faith, just as He called (brought) the universe into existence at cre-ation. In calling Abram the father of many nations, He was again calling something that was not, as being (as though it was) and thereby He was calling it into being.

It was now up to Abraham to get in harmony with God in this twofold way if this promise was to come to pass in his life.

Stage 1: He Received Life From God

God promised Abram he was a "father of many nations." He believed he received the promise even when it seemed impossible in the natural, and it transformed his hope, his image of the future, so that he had a confident expectation of the promise coming to pass, seeing it now through the eyes of faith:

> *Who, contrary to* [natural] *hope, in hope believed* [he received the promise and believed that he would see the promise mani-fested], *so that* [as a result] *he became the father of many nations, according to what was spoken* [the promise came to pass], *"So shall your descendants be"* (Romans 4:18).

When God spoke His word, His power was present with the promise to fulfill it, so when they believed they received the promise, they also received the power to bring it to pass.

Romans 4:19: "And not being weak in faith, he did not consider his own body, already dead (since he was about 100 years old), and the deadness of Sarah's womb."

Outwardly, Abraham's senses told him it was impossible, but he did not let unbelief dominate his heart, weakening his faith. Obviously he was aware of the natural impossibilities, contradictory symptoms and circumstances, just as our bodies tell us when we are sick. But he did not focus his attention on the problem, but on God's promise and power to perform it.

Romans 4:20-21: "He did not waver at the *promise of God* through unbelief, but was strengthened in [by] faith being fully convinced that what He had *promised* He was also *able to perform.*" He did not let doubts dominate his heart through preoccupation with what his senses told him, but instead he received strength and healing from God by faith. The basis of his faith was his confidence in God's ability and power to perform His word.

Sarah also "judged Him *faithful* who had *promised*" (Heb. 11:11). Notice that their confidence was based on: (1) God's character (His power and faithfulness) and (2) His promise. Base your faith upon God and His Word. To believe for healing, find the Scriptures that promise healing, and base your faith on them.

By meditating on God and His Word before praying the prayer of faith, they came to a firm belief that God was able to do what He said, and could be relied upon to do it. They knew El Shaddai was well able to do it, and so they made a settled decision to trust God.

Abraham and Sarah's faith was sustained by a confidence in God's character (power, love, and faithfulness). They had decided to believe the promise and trust God, against all natural hope. In the end, the only consideration was that God's promise had to be true, even though there was nothing going for them in the natural. Contradictory circumstances, natural realities, will speak to you, and you can't help but be aware of them, but balance that against God's Word, and His character and power that stands behind His Word. Remember that natural things, facts, are subject to change, but the spiritual things of God are eternal truths that will ultimately change present facts (see 2 Cor. 4:18).

Living in the presence of Him who gives life to the dead, Abraham was able to believe he received life, strength, to enable him to be fruitful. Likewise, Sarah believed she received the promise and thus received power to conceive, resulting in the birth, manifestation, of the promise, Isaac:

> By *faith* Sarah herself also **received strength** [**power**] *to conceive seed, and she bore a child when she was past the age, because she judged Him faithful who had promised* (Hebrews 11:11).

Thus the first step of faith is to believe that God gives life to the dead and believe we receive it from Him. We must reckon ourselves dead in our ability to fulfill it by our own power. We must come to the end of trusting ourselves, and come to God and receive His life. The first step of faith as we walk with God is believing we receive His gift of life, on the basis of His promise.

Having believed they received the power to conceive, Abraham and Sarah put corresponding actions to their faith! Nine months later, the promise was manifested in Isaac. During this time the answer, seed, was growing invisibly in her womb. Likewise, when you believe you receive your healing, it is growing in your spiritual womb. Although you can't see it, you have it! You are pregnant with God's healing power!

We now need to consider how their faith operated during this time, between receiving the promise (seed) and its manifestation, to help bring it forth into open, visible manifestation (Isaac's birth). Abraham and Sarah needed to continue in faith, believing for the power of God to work to renew and strengthen Sarah's body to be able to give birth. As the couple continued to believe, their bodies were continually infused with strength, for God's power continued to work in them.

Stage 2: Confession

This brings us to the second step of the faith process. In calling Abraham the "father of many nations," God called something that was not, as though it was. Abraham, walking before God did likewise, calling those things which be not, as being, calling things that do not yet exist (in the natural), as if they existed, and by doing this he was calling for them to come into manifestation.

Having believed he received the promise, Abraham confessed it as true by changing his name from Abram to Abraham—the father of many nations—calling himself what God had called him, getting into agreement with God. When God spoke His word to Abraham, calling that which was not into being, the power of God was present with the word to fulfill it, so when Abraham believed he received it and then confessed it, he put his "Amen" on it, and it had to come to pass:

Second Corinthians 1:20 can be interpreted in this way: All the promises of God in Christ are Yes, and in Him we utter the Amen resulting in the glory [manifestation] of God, through us.

So the second Stage of Faith is to walk in agreement with the God who "calls into being [manifestation] those things which do not [yet] exist [in the natural realm]" by speaking the word of faith (see Rom. 4:17).

In order to walk in agreement with God, Abraham had to confess the word. God called him Abraham, so he called himself Abraham. *Confession* means to say the same thing as God. He calls it done and having received it by faith, we too call it done. By faith he started *calling* himself Abraham, father of many nations. He had to say, I have received new life from God, and He has changed my name. Call me father of many nations, because that's who I am. He had to get in agreement with God and *call* those things that be not (yet manifested) as if they were. Like Abraham, we are to *confess*

God's promises to us as true before they are manifested, and thereby we call them forth into being, bringing them from the spiritual realm into the natural realm.

Abraham by faith, called himself "father" before he was a father, as if he was already a father, for in the Spirit it was true, causing God's power to be released to make him a father in the natural. Likewise, by calling ourselves "healed" before healing is manifest, we are not playing mind games. We are believing we have it in our spirits, and are calling for our healing to come forth into being, putting a demand on God's healing power to fulfill the word. In this way, we release His Spirit to bring our healing to pass in us. So, it is by our words of faith we bring our healing from our spirits into manifestation.

We keep God's power working in us to manifest strength (healing) by maintaining a strong, active faith by *meditation* on the Word, and thanksgiving, "...was strengthened in faith, *giving glory* to God, being *fully convinced* that what He had promised He was also able to perform" (Rom. 4:20-21).

As Abraham continued to feed his faith in meditation on God and His promise, and express his faith in thanksgiving (the voice of faith), his faith remained strong. As soon as he believed he received this strength by faith, he thanked God for it. Romans 4:19 can be translated: "he received strength by faith, giving glory to God."

Then as he continued to thank God for His promise, and for His power that was now in him bringing the promise to pass, he continued to be strengthened by God's power working in him. He kept the power of God active by keeping his faith switch turned on, continuing to believe and thanking God for the answer, "calling those things that do not exist as though they did." In faith, he gave thanks that God was bringing it to pass, praising His faithfulness and power to fulfill His promise. As he gave glory to God for fulfilling the promise, the switch stayed on and the power flowed.

Having decided to believe the promise, he did not meditate on the sense-evidence that breeds unbelief, focusing on his weakness and lack, but patiently continued to meditate on God's power and promise and to *rejoice* and give *thanks* to God for bringing it to pass. This protected his heart from thoughts that would have caused him to become weakened in faith and abandon the initial confidence he had when he believed he received the promise.

In this way he remained strong in faith, fully convinced that God was working and would surely fulfill His promise to him. As a result, he received his miraculous manifestation—Isaac! Thus "walking before God" Abraham (1) believed he received God's gift of life (healing) into his dying body, and (2) in agreement with God he confessed the promise, calling it into full manifestation. He (1) believed he *received* the promise and (2) *confessed* it.

Likewise, we are to walk in fellowship with God, operating in His kind of faith, who with the answer in His Spirit, looked into the darkness, emptiness, and void, and spoke forth the light: "Light be!" In the natural, it looked hopeless, yet God did not speak what was: "Oh, it's so dark and empty!" He saw the end result through the eyes of faith and spoke that into manifestation: calling those things that do not exist (in the natural) as (into) being. When Abraham believed the promise, it looked hopeless in the natural; their bodies as good as dead as far as having a child was concerned. But operating in the God-kind of faith, Abraham saw by faith the promise fulfilled and spoke it as done, calling it into being.

If your pet is not here (but out of sight), he still exists but in another place, so you call for, command, him to come to you, where you can see him. Although you can not see him, you believe he is real and so you call him into manifestation: "Here, Rover!" He is not "here" yet, but by calling him "as here," speaking the desired end result, you are calling for him to come "here" and thus causing him to be "here." Just crying and saying to yourself, *He is not here* achieves nothing!

Saying what you see in the natural changes nothing, but saying what you see in the spirit (as yours) will bring it into being. Likewise, even if we do not yet see our body healed, if healing is ours, because we believed we received it, we can call for it to come into manifestation. As the dog will respond and come, so as you call for healing power to come into manifestation, it will respond and come forth from your spirit: "Healing is mine. Healing come forth! God's healing power is working in me, driving out all sickness and making me whole."

The God-kind of faith calls what already exists in the spirit to come into the natural. How did God bring what is spiritual into the natural? By *words!* At creation, the Spirit was hovering, ready to perform the Word, so when God spoke the Word, the Spirit went forth with the Word to do it. So when God spoke and called for something in His Spirit to come forth, His Spirit moved and brought it forth into being.

When we speak words of faith based on His Word, calling forth something that is in our spirits that we have received from God, either in the new birth or in prayer, then God's Spirit in union with our spirits moves to bring it forth into being.

There is a *fight of faith* that we have to fight. Having (1) *laid hold* of our healing by faith, we have to stand our ground and (2) confess our faith, resisting any enemy who would try to steal it.

First Timothy 6:12 says, "Fight the good fight of faith, [1] lay hold on eternal life [which includes healing] to which you were also called and [2] have confessed the good confession...."

Tricia, mentioned in the Introduction, had a diseased and blackened inner ear and was in extreme pain. She pressed in to the Lord to receive her healing. She walked the floor for hours, confessing God's Word aloud over herself and rebuking satan. She knew that Jesus had paid for her healing with His stripes. Knowing this, she was able to stand and continue to do this despite the pain. She knew the importance of speaking out loud to proclaim her faith and command the enemy to take his hands off her body, bought at the price of Jesus' blood. For a couple of weeks nothing seemed to change, but she was determined and confident that God was with her.

Also, she had to take authority in the name of Jesus over a spirit of fear that accompanied the pain. At last she was gloriously free from fear. Then her faith could fully function. But the pain still continued for a time, while she continued to make a good confession each day and night. Then the pain stopped, and when she went to her appointment with the specialist, he looked very carefully and said, "I don't know why your doctor sent you to me, this is a textbook ear." Tricia told me that for years afterward, whenever she saw her doctor, he would ask about her ear. She always replied, "I told you God would heal me." He said, "I was very worried about that ear…"

3. Commanding Sickness to Be Removed

As well as calling our healing forth and commanding healing into our bodies, we can also command any sickness that remains to be removed. In Matthew 16:19, Jesus gives us the authority to bind or forbid (sickness and satan) as well as loose or release God's healing power.

We can say, "Healing *be!*" and "Mountain, be removed!" (see Mark 11:23). We speak against the negative to remove it. Jesus described the process of faith in Mark:

> *Have faith in God* [operate in the God-kind of faith]. *For assuredly, I say to you, whoever says to this mountain* [of sickness that is standing in the way, blocking our healing], *'Be removed and be cast into the sea,' and does not doubt in his heart* [literally: does not let doubt enter into his heart], *but believes that those things he says will be done* [come to pass], *he will have* [manifested] *whatever he says. Therefore I say to you, whatever things you desire, when you pray, believe that you receive them, and you will have them. And whenever you stand praying* [ready to believe you receive] *if you have anything against anyone, forgive him, that your Father in heaven may also forgive you your trespasses* (Mark 11:22-25).

We must speak to the mountain (of sickness) in the way of our healing, rather than begging God to remove it. When we speak the faith command, God's power is released against it to remove it. It may look immovable but it's nothing compared to God's power! Say, "Sickness be removed from my body and don't come back!"

Jesus promises us that God's Spirit will back up our command and manifest what we say, whether commanding healing or the removal of sickness—He will have (manifested) whatever he says but only if he "believes that those things he says will be done."

Thus we can only successfully speak the answer (healing) forth, if we are in faith, having already believed we have received it in our spirits. This is confirmed by the requirement of not letting doubt enter our hearts. This implies that in Mark 11:23, we have entered the realm of having believed we have received our healing, but there is a danger of letting unbelief into the heart, from looking at the mountain (of sickness) that still remains in our bodies.

Therefore Mark 11:23 tells us that having believed we have received our healing, we must maintain our position of faith, protecting our heart from the entrance of doubts, and speak our healing into manifestation, commanding healing to come into our bodies and commanding sickness to leave, believing that what we say will be done for we will have what we say.

So before implementing Mark 11:23 by speaking the answer forth, believing it will come to pass, we must know we have it in the spirit. Thus we must first of all have received it from God—when God calls something forth, He automatically has it in His Spirit, as at creation, but we can only speak out what we have already received from God. Therefore, after Jesus tells us how to give a faith command in Mark 11:23, He tells us in Mark 11:24 how to get into position to do it:

Therefore [in order to satisfy the heart condition required by v23] *I say to you, whatever things you ask* [such as healing] *when you pray, believe that you receive them* [into your spirit], *and you will have them* [see them manifested physically].

Notice that *having* the answer is mentioned in verses 23 and 24: "you will have them" (v.24) ..."he will have whatever he says" (v.23).

The first key to having them is believing we receive them from God. The second key to having them manifested is speaking them forth, believing that what we say will come to pass that God will do them, for "we will have whatever we say." If we know we have received healing, then we can speak healing into our bodies, and command sickness to be removed, "Body, be healed! Sickness, be gone, in Jesus name!" and we will have what we say, if we believe that our words will come to pass through the power of God working with us.

Mark 11:24 says if we believe we receive it, then we will have it. But Mark 11:23 clarifies that this is not automatic, for it says that we will have what we *say*. Thus *having it* does not just depend on *receiving* it by faith, but also *saying* (confessing) it by faith. It only promises that we will have it, if we *say* it, believing what we say will come to pass. In other words, we will manifestly have the healing we have received by faith, if we continue in faith, calling it forth with the word of faith and commanding the removal of sickness.

Therefore to *have* something in manifestation, we must:

1. Receive it from God through the prayer of faith, and then,

2. Speak it forth by the word of faith, commanding anything in the way to be removed, believing that what we say shall come to pass.

Thus we will *have* what we *say*, if we believe it; that is, if we have believed we received it, and if we believe it is coming to pass into manifestation through our words. Thus, having received something through prayer, there must also be corresponding words and actions to help bring it to pass, or else the power of God may become inactive through our passivity or neglect, especially if we allow doubts to enter into our hearts about whether we really received it, turning the switch of faith off, and thus short-circuiting the power of God that brings the manifestation, as Mark 11:23 warns can happen.

Mark 11:23-25 describes the operation of the God-kind of faith using reverse logic, similar to the logical order in Romans 10:13:15. Mark 11:23 says that to have the answer, we must say it, believing that what we say will be done. Therefore, to do this, says verse 24, we must first believe we receive it in prayer. But to do this successfully, says verse 25, you must walk in forgiveness, or else your prayer will be hindered.

To put this process in chronological order, to *have it* we must:

1. Forgive any sins committed against us (v.25).

2. Then we will be able to believe we receive it in our spirits (v.24).

3. Then we will be able to speak it forth from our spirits, believing that it will come to pass, trusting the Spirit of God to do it (v.23).

So we've seen that having believed we have received our healing, we should thank God for it, and in the name of Jesus *call* God's healing power forth into manifestation, and *command* all sickness to be removed into the sea—out of sight, never to return.

Mark 11:23-24 promises that we will have the answer manifest in our bodies if we believe we receive it in our spirits, and then use our God-given authority to speak it into our bodies in Jesus name, believing in God's promise, that He will bring to pass what we say.

4. Declare Our Beliefs to Protect Our Hearts From Unbelief

During the time between receiving and having the manifestation, we must *defend* our position of faith against attack from doubts—thoughts (either from satan or from natural circumstances and reasonings) contradicting God's promise that we have received and that it is coming to pass. This is necessary, for as we saw from Mark 11:23, if doubts dominate and are allowed to enter the heart creating unbelief there, the power of God producing our healing will be shut down.

Proverbs 4:23 says, "Keep [guard] your heart with all diligence for out of it spring [flow] the issues [forces] of life [including God's healing power]" (see also John 7:37). We do this by putting God's Word first:

> *My son, give attention to my words; incline your ear to my sayings. Do not let them depart from your eyes; keep them in the midst of your heart. For they are life to those who find them and* **health** *to* **all** *their* **flesh** (Proverbs 4:20-22).

According to the Parable of the Sower (see Mark 4) our hearts are like a garden where God wants to bring forth good fruit (healing), through His Word (seed) of healing being planted (received) and then growing in us to produce a full visible manifestation, the full-grown plant. It also warns of things that can prevent this from happening if proper care is not taken. The key to the Parable, to us becoming good soil is: "He who has ears, let him hear [and keep on hearing] the Word." As we put the Word first, by hearing and speaking it, the faith roots of our healing seed will be strong, enabling it to continue working under pressure. We will also be watering the seed of healing power in us, stimulating its growth, and weeding the soil, guarding our seed by removing any doubts, desires, and distractions hindering its growth.

We must not only enter the realm of believing we receive when we pray, but we must also stand our ground in faith, maintaining our position of faith that we have believed we received our healing when we prayed, or when hands were laid on us. This is keeping the faith switch turned on. After taking possession of new ground in our Promised Land by faith (believing we receive it), we must now keep (hold) it by faith. It takes diligence in the Word to enter into rest, possess the land, just as it took diligence for Israel to possess her land (see Heb. 4:11-12). But it also takes diligence to remain in the land, as it did for Israel, because our position of faith will be attacked by enemies trying to get us to abandon our position.

STAND IN FAITH

After praying in faith, doubts may come to our minds attacking God's faithfulness to His Word, questioning if He really gave us healing power when we prayed. We must learn to resist these attacks, *holding* our ground (our position of faith), *standing* firm on the Word of God, and *defending* our positions with God's Word, "Watch, *stand* fast in the faith, be brave, be strong" (I Cor. 16:13).

> *Finally, my brethren, be strong in the Lord and in the power of His might. Put on the whole armor of God, that you may be able to stand against the wiles of the devil. . . .that you may be able to withstand in the evil day, and having done all, to stand. Stand therefore. . .* (Ephesians 6:10-14)

> *Submit to God* [and His Word, by believing you receive His promise of healing]. ***Resist*** *the devil and he will flee from you* (James 4:7).

Resist *him, steadfast in the faith* (I Peter 5:9). We resist satan by maintaining our position of faith in the promise, having believed we received it.

We must be ready to defend our position of faith and the beliefs that undergird it, so the doubts will not succeed in causing us to abandon this position. When doubts arise that question if we have received, perhaps from symptoms of sickness or pain, they must be responded to immediately and dealt with decisively, or else we will start entertaining thoughts that will eventually cause us to drift away from believing we have received when we prayed, even to the point of denouncing that belief, causing God's power in us to be shut down.

We attained our position of faith on the basis of the four beliefs we've studied in this book. Knowing and maintaining these beliefs about God (His will, nature, gift, and method) will enable us to *continue* to believe we have received, so that God's power will *continue* to work healing in us, until we are fully satisfied with the fruit produced. On the other hand, the doubts that come to move us off our position of faith will attack one or more of these four beliefs. You may have thoughts such as: *Maybe it's not God's will to heal me now. I can't presume God gave me anything when I prayed. I don't feel any different, so I didn't receive healing. Nothing happened when hands were laid on me.*

Therefore, in order to *defend* our position of faith from attack, we must be ready to defend these essential beliefs that undergird it. First, this requires us *knowing* these beliefs well and knowing the Scriptures that these beliefs are based upon so that we will not only be strong enough in faith to believe we receive our healing, but we are also able to maintain our position of faith when attacked by doubts.

Second, in order to successfully defend these beliefs, we must *declare* out loud what we believe—rather than just thinking it. *Confessing* our beliefs helps us to defend them effectively and thus to maintain our position of faith. When doubts arise to question whether the laying on of hands was beneficial, we should confess:

> God's will is my healing, and He is a liberal Giver of healing power, so when hands were laid on me in Jesus' name, God gave me healing power, and I believed I received it right then. So now His healing power is continually working mightily in my body driving out all sickness and making me whole. Thank You, Lord.

We must not abandon our belief that healing power was given and administered to our bodies the instant that hands were laid upon us. We should also use the Scriptures that support these beliefs, for we overcome by our *words* agreeing with God's *Word* (see Rev. 12:11). This is how Jesus consistently dealt with thoughts sent by satan to attack and undermine His position of faith in God's Word (see Luke 4:1-13). In response to every thought of satan, Jesus *said*: "It is written!" (see Matt. 4:4,7,10). This is His definitive example to us of how to stand and overcome in spiritual warfare. He used no other method to overcome satan. There is no other way revealed in the Bible to fight this fight of faith! We must follow His example and *speak out* what we believe, along with the Scriptures that support those beliefs, when faced with thoughts that question if we received when we prayed. We must resist natural doubts and the devil's lies by declaring out loud God's Word concerning healing (see James 4:7).

When we speak the Word against the doubts, they will dissipate and disappear, and we will find it easy to remain loyal to our beliefs. Thus we must defend our position of faith by speaking God's Word, declaring out loud what we know about our Father, using the Scriptures that support these beliefs and that formed them within us.

Our response to any doubts should be immediate so that they have no time to play upon our minds and enter our hearts. Scriptures are to become a sword in our mouth, which we take out of the belt of truth—the truth of God wrapped around our hearts—and use to defend our position: "take...the sword of the Spirit, which is the [spoken] word of God" (Eph. 6:17). This will cause all doubts to retreat.

CONCLUSION

From the moment that we believe we receive, our confession must be the result of what we believe. We must now identify more with our healing than with the sickness. We are now to walk by faith, what we believe, not by sight, what we physically see or feel. After we have received healing power by faith, we must patiently stand by faith, maintaining our position in this realm of faith by continuing to believe that we have received God's healing power, until we are satisfied with the fruit, the manifestation of healing, produced by it. We help to keep the switch of faith turned on by giving voice to our faith. We *give thanks* to God for His healing power, *confessing* our faith that we have received it and that it is now working mightily in us, for this will keep the healing power active and working in us!

STIR UP GOD'S HEALING POWER GIFT

First Timothy 4:14-15 says:

> *Do not **neglect** the **gift** that is **in you**, which was **given** to you by prophecy with the laying on of the hands of the eldership. **Meditate** on these things; **give yourself** entirely to them, that your progress may be **evident** [manifest] to all.*

God had given Timothy a gift through the laying on of hands, and Paul tells Timothy what he should do with it so that this gift becomes active and fruitful in him.

Although the gift was not healing power, the same principles apply. In Second Timothy 1:6, Paul talks to Timothy a second time about this gift:

> *I remind you [again] to stir up [fan into flame] the gift of God, which is in you through the laying on of my hands.*

We often need reminding because we get too taken up with the problems. The first time he said that he must not neglect God's gift in him. The second time he explains this negative statement by giving the positive equivalent, saying that he must stir up God's gift in him. To stir up means to arouse from dormancy into activity, as you would fan a fading flame into new life. The gift was dormant, because Timothy had neglected it, but it was still in him, and it was up to him to stir it up into action again. God's healing power can be in us and yet lie within us dormant and inactive if we neglect it; but we do not lose it, for when God gives a gift, He does not take it away, "for the gifts and calling of God are irrevocable" (Rom. 11:29). This gift did not leave Timothy just because he did not keep it active. Healing power does not leave us after a time of inactivity.

However, for this gift to be productive in Timothy, it was vital that he did not neglect (ignore or be careless of) it any longer. God may give a person a gift, and yet it can lie dormant or inactive. It does not manifest just because it is present. So it is with God's healing power. It can be present in our bodies but lie dormant. When hands were laid on us, God's healing power was administered to us, but what we do with it after that is up to us. Just because it has been given does not guarantee that we will be healed. We must do something with the healing power once it has been administered to us if it is to remain active and manifest the healing we desire.

Once a gift has been given to us, it is ours, and so it is our responsibility—not God's—to keep it active and working. If neglected, it will become dormant. Many will not benefit from the healing power in them, until they give it the attention needed for it to continue to work once it has been obtained. We are not to ask God to stir it up, we must do it. Notice that Timothy could stir up his gift anytime that he desired, but if he chose to ignore it, it would remain unproductive.

Likewise, God's gift of healing power will lie dormant in us, until we choose to stir it up. If we neglect it, there is nothing God can do to activate it. Many fail to be healed, because when they do not quickly see or feel the desired results, they became unbelieving, and this causes the healing power to become dormant in them. We must not neglect it, but repent and stir it up again, fanning it into a brightly burning flame. When we make healing power active, it will begin to work to drive out sickness and to affect a healing and a cure in us.

Spiritual things will lie neglected and dormant in us until:

1. We become aware of their presence.

2. We take the responsibility to stir up what we have been given.

One reason people neglect healing power is because they focus on the sickness, forgetting the healing power that they received. Therefore, they become unaware of its presence in them. The first thing they need is to remember that they received it. Paul twice reminded Timothy that the gift was present, even reminding him how and when it was given him, before telling him to stir it up. We must first be convinced that it is present in us, before we can stir it up. It is not enough just to generally believe in divine healing.

We must personally believe that we received healing power when hands were laid on us, and therefore know that we have healing power present in us. Then we are ready to stir it into activity. When we believe this, we should think, talk, and walk differently from those who just believe generally in healing; this will activate the healing power and keep it working in us.

We may know the gift is present but still neglect it because we do not give it the attention it deserves and requires to keep it active, for we focus all our attention on other things—the sickness or other problems. It is OK to give attention to problems, but not to the extent that we neglect the very thing that will help us—God's healing power. Neglected power is dormant, idle, inactive power. But if we stir God's power into activity by giving it due attention, it will heal us.

How can we stir the gift of God up? What attention does it need?

Look again at First Timothy 4:14-15.

1. We must continue to *meditate*, think, fix our hearts on God's gift of healing power, reminding ourselves of how it was supplied through the cross, how it was administered to us, the four key beliefs and supporting Scriptures that enabled us to believe we received it and how it is working in us now to drive out sickness and heal us.

2. We are to give ourselves wholly to it. This means our lives are built around it, so it should show in our words and actions. This starts by *talking* about it and *thanking* God for giving us His healing power that is working mightily in us. Then it cannot lie dormant, but will keep working in us until we are satisfied with the fruit produced. By confessing the promise we activate the power.

If you do these things, the gift will become active and fruitful, "your progress will appear [be manifest] to all." *All will see* that you have profited from God's healing power! If you give yourself to bodybuilding, your progress will soon appear to all. Likewise, if you give yourself to God's healing power *all will see* you have profited from it by the health it produces in you. Timothy profited originally when the gift was given to him, but it did not appear to all until he stirred it up by thinking, talking, thanking, and living it. If healing power is valuable enough for Jesus to die for it, then it is valuable enough for us not to neglect it. We need to give it our proper attention so that it can do in us what it is designed to do—manifest our healing so it appears obvious to all.

If you know that you have received healing power through the laying on of hands, then stir it up into action by saying:

> God's healing power is now working mightily in my body driving out all sickness and manifesting a healing and cure in me. I know this, because hands were laid on me according to Mark 16. This promises my recovery started the very moment hands were laid on me, due to the immediate transmission of healing power into me in confirmation of the Gospel of Christ. His Word declares healing power has been made freely available through Christ's death and resurrection, is made present by the spoken word, and is imparted by hands to the sick to work their full recovery. So when hands were laid on me, healing power was given to me and is now working in me.

God's healing power that starts working in you the moment you believe you receive it is just as powerful today as in the days of Jesus when it was well able to heal all kinds of sickness and disease!

Remember, the promise of Jesus to you is that if you believe you receive your healing when you pray: *"You will have them"* manifested (Mark 11:24), as long as you keep believing, not allowing doubt into your heart, and *speak* [call forth] your healing and *command* the removal of the sickness, for it is also true that, *you will have what you say* (see Mark 11:23).

HEALING TRUTHS

- As God's children, healing belongs to us. It is bought and paid for by the atonement of Christ. Through the New Covenant in His blood, the Lord is our Healer. Healing is freely available to receive.

- When we pray the prayer of faith for our healing, we believe we receive healing power from the Lord, our Healer (see Mark 11:24).

- After the prayer of faith, we must hold fast our position of faith, believing we have received healing power, and that it is actively working in us to drive out all sickness and making us whole.

- In the time between receiving the answer and seeing it manifested, we are to express our faith through our words, by:

    1. Giving *thanks* to God for His gift of healing power.

    2. *Confessing* the Word, *calling, commanding* our healing to come forth. Having *received* God's healing power into our body, the next step is to speak it into manifestation.

    3. *Commanding sickness* and *fear* to be *removed*.

    4. *Declaring* your *beliefs* to protect our heart from unbelief

- In this way we *stir up* into activity God's gift of healing power within us.

- This divine gift of healing power is well able to drive out any sickness and restore our health, but we are responsible to keep it actively working in us by keeping our faith switch turned on.

Appendix A

GOD'S METHODS OF HEALING

There are a number of different methods, by which God imparts healing to our bodies.

1. *The Spoken Word (see Luke 7:1-10; Mark 11:23).* God's healing power can be spoken into someone's body and sickness rebuked, using words like: "Be healed. Receive your healing now in the name of Jesus. Sickness, I command you to be removed now." In these cases, healing Power is ministered to a sick body without there being any physical contact—often it happens over a distance.

2. *The Prayer of Faith (see Mark 11:24).* Having heard and believed God's promises, we can simply come to God in prayer and believe we receive His healing power into our bodies. In this method, we receive healing directly from God, rather than it being ministered to us. Someone can help us do this by praying with us in agreement (see Matt. 18:18-20), or by praying for us, but we still need to receive the answer from God.

There is a difference between laying hands on someone to minister God's healing power to them, and laying hands on them to identify with them and asking God in prayer to heal them. In the former case, healing power is transmitted through the hands; but in the latter case, it is received directly from God through prayer; the hands are incidental. Therefore, receiving healing from God through the prayer of faith does not require touch.

3.   *Touch.* The ministry of Jesus not only reveals this is a God-ordained method of healing, but also that this is His primary method. In it, a physical contact is established between the sick person and the anointing, upon a minister or within a cloth. Then, by faith, God's healing anointing (power) is transmitted into him, flowing according to the spiritual law of contact and transmission. Thus healing power is imparted by means of or through a believing touch.

This contact or *touch of faith* can be established in three ways:

1. The touch of faith is usually done through the *laying on of hands.* This is when an anointed minister lays his hands upon the sick person in faith, believing that God's healing power will then flow into the person. The recipient should also believe this and receive the healing power. As you will see in this Appendix through biblical examples, Jesus primarily used this method to heal the sick.

2. Second, the touch of faith can be also done by the *hands* of the one needing healing. This is when the sick person reaches out to touch a minister of healing, who has the healing anointing upon him, and receives this healing power by faith, causing it to flow into his body. Many received their healing from Jesus by simply touching Him, and by faith receiving the flow of His healing power into their bodies.

This is how the woman with the issue of blood received her healing (Mark 5:24-34, see also Mark 3:10, 6:54-56; Luke 6:17-19; Matthew 14:34-36). These accounts show that the healing power upon Jesus was available to all to come and receive from Him, so that when they touched Him in faith, believing they received healing power, that power flowed freely from Him into them and healed them.

They had faith to do this because of His consistent proclamation that it was Jubilee time (the acceptable Year of the Lord), the time of grace for all, when you can claim your freedom and restoration. Jesus proclaimed that He had been anointed with healing power, that it was upon Him for them to be healed and delivered (see Luke 4:18-21). He also proclaimed the Good News of the Kingdom of God, which includes forgiveness and healing, and that Good News is that: "the kingdom of God is [now] at hand" (Mark 1:14-15; Matt. 4:17). This means these blessings of the Kingdom were being offered freely and were available for all to receive, so all they had to do is just reach out with the hand of faith and take them.

They did this with God's healing power. Jesus told them that He was anointed or covered with it and invited them to lay hold of it, so they came to Him and made contact with that power by laying their hands on Him, pulling that power out from Him by their faith. God is still holding out His healing power to us as a free gift, for us to come and lay hold of it by faith. It is still "at hand" for us to come with boldness and take, receive, it with our hand of faith.

We see in the Gospels that many received healing this way. It was especially helpful when there were multitudes around Jesus and there would not have been enough time for Jesus to lay hands on them all individually. In this method, individual prayer is not required so it is quicker—they approached Jesus from all directions as He was standing or walking and just took their healing from Him without interrupting Him or taking up His time any further: "He healed many, so that as many as had afflictions pressed about Him to *touch* Him" (Mark 3:10). "The whole multitude sought to *touch* Him, for *power* went out from Him and healed them all" (Luke 6:19).

They did not even have to touch His *person*, for many received healing by just touching His *clothing*. This was possible because *cloth* can both *store* and *conduct* healing power.

Christ's clothing was saturated with the healing power upon Him. Notice in Mark 5:24-34 that the woman with the issue of blood did not touch Jesus Himself, but only touched the hem of His garment, "...she came *behind Him* in the crowd and *touched* His *garment*" She actually just touched the *hem* of His *garment* (see Matt. 9:20; Luke 8:44).

*For she said, "If only I may touch His **clothes**, I shall be made well."*
Immediately the fountain of her blood was dried up, and she felt in her
body that she was healed (Mark 5:27-29).

She was not alone in this:

Wherever He entered, into villages, cities, or the country, they laid the
*sick in the marketplaces, and begged Him that they might just **touch the***
***hem of His garment**. And as many as **touched** Him were made well*
(Mark 6:56).

. . .they came to the land of Gennesaret. And when the men of that place
recognized Him, they sent out into all that surrounding region, brought
*to Him all who were sick, and begged Him that they might only **touch***
***the hem of His garment**. And as many as **touched it** were made per-*
fectly well (Matthew 14:34-36).

Thus the anointing that was in and upon Jesus was also in and on His
clothing; when someone touched His clothing in faith, believing they
would receive healing, the power flowed into them.

An outer cloak or mantle upon a man of God is a symbol of his anointing and authority. In fact, the Hebrew word for mantle means power and
strength. To be anointed is to be clothed with power from on high (see
Luke 24:49), just as the Holy Spirit came upon Jesus and clothed or covered Him with power at His baptism. Therefore it is fitting that the anointing also abides in the clothing of an anointed one.

When Elijah threw his mantle over Elisha, it signified that he was to be
anointed as a prophet (see 1 Kings 19:16,19). Elijah used this mantle, representing the anointing or power of God upon him, to smite the waters of
Jordan and divide them so they could walk over on dry land (see 2 Kings
2:8). His mantle had absorbed the power of God upon him, so when he
smote the waters in faith, that miracle-working power was released. Elisha's
request was that he would inherit a double-portion of Elijah's anointing or
spirit (v.9). Elisha did receive it, for the anointing on Elijah was transferred
to Elisha (see 2 Kings 2:9-15).

It's instructive to see how this transfer of anointing (mantle) happened:

1. Elisha saw Elijah ascend.

2. He saw his mantle descend.

3. He tore up his own clothes.

4. He took up the mantle of Elijah.

5. He used it to divide the waters as Elijah had done.

6. The other prophets then realized that the spirit (anointing) on Elijah was now resting upon Elisha.

This confirms the mantle worn by a prophet represented the anointing upon him and his mantle was saturated with this anointing.

When Jesus, the Greater than Elijah, "ascended on high," He also gave His anointing, including His healing power, to His disciples, for "He gave gifts [anointings] to men" (see Eph. 4:8-12).

Like Elisha we need to be faithful disciples:

• Through the eyes of faith, we must see Jesus ascend on high.

• We must see the Spirit (our mantle or anointing to minister) descend, for we see Jesus pouring out the gift of the Spirit upon us.

• We must reject our own clothes (ministering in our own authority and power).

• By faith we must receive (take hold) of the mantle (authority and anointing) He gives us.

• By faith we are to release this power (anointing) against any sickness, and thus drive it away.

• Then people will see that a measure of the same Spirit that was upon Jesus is also upon us.

As God clothed Jesus with a mantle or cloak of power, so Jesus also clothes us with His Spirit upon us.

We can see why people touched His clothing to receive healing. The outer garment of Christ represented the authority and anointing power of

God upon Him, and so by touching it, those who believed He was the Anointed One, believed they were touching, laying hold of, the power He had proclaimed was available for them. When they laid hold of His garment, by faith they were really laying hold of His anointing, and this anointing stored in the garment flowed into them and healed them. Their actions showed that they believed in Him as the Anointed One and they were laying hold of and receiving that anointing.

When Elisha laid hold of Elijah's mantle, he was really laying hold of his anointing. He took it and put it to work, released it by faith. Just as Elisha applied this power against the problem, the waters, standing in his way, believing that it would drive them away, so we must receive God's healing power and put it to work in our bodies, by believing and confessing that it is driving all our sickness away. Then the way will be opened for us to move forward again in our lives, without sickness blocking our way.

We saw that since the clothing of Christ contained the healing power that was upon Him, people could receive their healing by laying their hands on His clothing. In this way they set up a point of physical contact with this healing power, through which it could be transmitted, if they believed they received it. It is interesting that the people specifically touched "the Hem [border] of His garment."

This was a sign of humility and faith in Jesus as their Messiah-King, for the way a person should approach a king with a petition, was to prostrate himself and touch the hem of his robe (the symbol of the king's authority and power) acknowledging and bowing before his authority and requesting that the king use his power on his behalf. Thus they were coming to Jesus, the Messiah-King, bowing to His Lordship, and requesting His healing power for their bodies.

They had a scriptural basis for this, from a well-known prophecy of the Messiah: "The Sun of Righteousness shall arise with *healing* in His *wings* [rays]" (Mal. 4:2).

This says the Messiah will radiate healing power like the sun! This power is for all believers just as the warmth and light of the sun is for all, especially those who go outside to receive it. But the word translated *wings* is the same word that is used for the corners or borders of an outer garment. For example, when Ruth says to Boaz: "Take your maidservant under your wing" (Ruth 3:9), this could also translate as: Spread the corner of your garment over your maidservant. She was asking him to cover and protect her with his authority and power symbolized by his garment (a marriage proposal), so that she would come under the shadow of his wings—just as we can abide under the shadow of the Lord's wings (see Ps. 91).

So there was a tradition (from Malachi 4:2) that the Royal Messiah would have healing in the borders of His garment. This is confirmed by Psalm 133:2, which is a prophecy of the anointing (oil) upon Christ our High Priest, greater than Aaron: "It is like the precious *oil* upon the head, running down on the beard, the beard of Aaron, running down on the *edge* of his *garments*."

Aaron is a type of Christ anointed by God. Notice this anointing can *flow*. Also notice that this *oil of life* is not just on the Head (Christ), but is meant to be shared with the whole Body, or Church). Reading this literally tells us the anointing poured out on Messiah, would come upon all His clothing, even down to its borders. Thus the hem of this King's garment symbolizes the place from where His power (anointing) flows (when David cut off the edge of Saul's Robe in First Samuel 24, he was convicted that he had acted against the anointing of God). This helps to explain why they came to Jesus and touched the hem of His garment expecting to receive their healing.

We get more insight into what was going on spiritually when people touched the hem of Christ's garment, by looking at God's instructions for making this outer garment in Numbers 15:38-40:

> *Speak to the children of Israel: Tell them to make tassels* [or fringes, tzitzit] *on the corners* [borders or wings] *of their garments throughout their generations, and to put a blue thread in the tassels of the corners. And you shall have the tassel, that you may look upon it and remember all the commandments of the Lord and do them, and that you may not follow the harlotry to which your own heart and your*

own eyes are inclined, and that you may remember and do all My com-
mandments, and be holy for your God (see also Deut. 22:12).

This is how the Jewish prayer shawls, tallit, are still made today.

The garment represents God's covering presence and power. When the
man went outside, it would protect him from the elements. *Tallit* means lit-
tle tent, so that when it is pulled over the head, it forms a private sanctuary
in which one meets with God. Here one shuts the door on everything else
and focuses on God. As Jesus said in Matthew 6:6:

> *When you pray, go into your* [private] *room, and when you have shut*
> *your door, pray to your Father who is in the Secret Place* [in the
> Spirit]; *and your Father who sees in secret will reward you openly.*

Coming under the prayer shawl is a picture of dwelling, spiritually, in
the secret place of the Most High, in His very presence, under His the covering of His wings (see Ps. 91:1-4).

A outer garment is made of a rectangular piece of cloth with tassels at-
tached to the corners, wings. According to Numbers 15:38-40, these tassels
represent the words of God and must be clearly seen, so as to be a constant
reminder to the man wearing it. Thus, wherever he walks he sees the tassels
and is reminded to walk according to God's Word and not his own ways.
When he prays under the shawl, he is wrapped around in the tassels, reminding him to wrap himself about with God's words and promises.

The threads of the tassels are white (signifying *purity*), except for one
blue thread (signifying *faithfulness*). This shows forth the fact that God's
faithfulness stands behind all His words, so that we can put all our faith in
them. Jesus criticized the Pharisees for, "to be seen by men...They make
their phylacteries broad and enlarge the borders [and tassels] of their garments" (Matt. 23:5). They wore massive tassels to show off how they were
more obedient to the Word than other men. They missed the point! The
tassels were meant to help produce humble submission to the Word, not
self-righteous pride.

The tassels are like feathers projecting from the end of the wings or
corners of this Jewish outer garment. Therefore the hem, border, of His

garment included these tassels. Jesus, as a law-abiding Jew, would have worn an outer garment with these tassels. It is these tassels, representing God's faithfulness and Word, that are the vital parts of the hem of this garment, for God's power works through His Word. We lay hold of God's power by trusting and receiving His Word. His power is in His Word, so when we receive His Word into us, we also receive His power.

When the people came to Jesus and bowed down to touch the hem of His garment, these tassels are what they were seeking to touch. The tassels of the Messiah represented all of God's faithful words, commands and promises, fulfilled in Him. These promises included healing power for all the sick.

Therefore, in laying hold of these tassels, they were taking hold by faith of the promises of God, now fulfilled in Christ. They were trusting in His faithfulness to the Word He preached, that He was their Messiah, Savior, and Healer. In taking hold of His tassels, they were putting all their trust in His Word of healing, and as a result they received, believed, His healing power into their bodies.

When Jesus came the first time, He wore the mantle of a prophet. He now wears priestly garments (see Rev. 1:12-18). When He returns, He will wear the robe that shows forth His full authority and power as King, "He has on His robe and on His thigh a name written: King of kings and Lord of lords" (Rev. 19:16). In each case His outer garments show forth the authority and power of the office in which He stands.

Having seen that people were healed by touching Christ's clothing, because it had absorbed the anointing that was upon Him, we now come to the third way people can be healed through *touch*:

3. Healing through anointed prayer cloths. This is an extension of the method of touch, based on the fact that certain materials, such as cloth, can store and conduct the healing anointing power of God. Therefore a cloth that has been in contact with the healing anointing, perhaps through having hands laid upon it, can be taken to the sick and placed upon their bodies, and then the healing power stored in these cloths will flow into their bodies to drive out the sickness and heal them—if this power is received by faith. Thus the healing power flows to the sick, according to the law of contact and transmission, in two stages. First of all it is transmitted from the minister to the cloth, and then from the cloth to the sick body.

This is what happened in Acts 19:11-12:

> God worked unusual miracles by the hands of Paul, so that even hand-kerchiefs [cloths] or aprons [clothing] were brought from his body to the sick, and the diseases left them and the evil spirits went out of them.

God's healing power still works the same way today. Cloths can be used to get the anointing to someone sick, when it is not possible for them to go to a healing service and also not possible to go and lay hands on them. It is important that along with the cloth, they are given instruction on how the cloth contains God's healing power, and how to believe they receive it when the cloth is laid upon them.

Flesh, blood, and bone can also store and conduct healing power, for otherwise it could not be transmitted through the laying on of hands, or go into a body and abide there to drive out sickness and produce healing in every kind of body part. An incident from Elisha's ministry demonstrates that bones in particular can store healing power. Having received the double portion of Elijah's spirit, the number of recorded miracles by Elisha was twice as many as Elijah, save one. However, after his death, he did one more miracle through his anointing and this made the doubling exact!

> Elisha died, and they buried him. ...So it was, as they were burying a man, that suddenly they spied a band of raiders; and they put the man in the tomb of Elisha; and when the man was let down and touched the bones of Elisha, he revived and stood on his feet (2 Kings 13:20-21).

Evidently Elisha's bones had absorbed God's anointing upon him during his lifetime and had continued to store it even after his death, so that when a dead man touched Elisha's bones, the anointing in the bones was transmitted into his body and it brought him back to life and healed him! Our bodies and clothes can be so saturated with healing power, so that when people believe we are anointed and touch us, or our clothes, they will be healed.

Proportion of Times

We have been looking at the various methods by which God's healing power is administered to the sick. It is interesting to classify all the healings of Jesus and the apostles according to these different methods. I believe that these examples of healing were given to show the variety of ways by which God heals us, His ordained ways of healing. I also believe that the proportion of times each method is used in these recorded accounts gives us the approximate proportion of times it was used in His ministry.

Therefore, if one method dominates in these accounts, we can deduce that it was and is God's normal method of administering healing power. If we look at all the accounts of healing that describe the method used, then it is clear that most healings happened through *touch*, and that this contact was usually made through the laying on of hands. Thus the normal method for ministering healing power is through the laying on of hands.

Jesus believed in the laying on of hands, and often used it to administer healing power to the sick:

1. *The Raising of the Widow's Son* (see Luke 7:11-17). "Then He came and touched the open coffin...And He said, 'Young man, I say to you, arise.' So he who was dead sat up and began to speak." He commanded his spirit back into his body, and healed him from whatever had caused his premature death through touch.

2. *The Man born Blind* (see John 9:1-7). "When He had said these things, He spat on the ground and made clay with the saliva; and He anointed the eyes of the blind man with the clay."

3. *The Woman with a Spirit of Infirmity* (see Luke 13:10-17). "Behold, there was a woman who had a spirit of infirmity eighteen years, and was bent over and could in no way raise herself up. But when Jesus saw her, He called her to Him and said to her, 'Woman, you are loosed from your infirmity.' And He laid His hands on her, and immediately she was made straight, and glorified God." First of all, He took authority over the evil spirit

by His words. Then through His hands, He ministered healing power to her body to restore her health.

4. *The Afflicted Boy* (see Matthew 17:14-21; Mark 9:14-29; Luke 9:37-43). "Jesus rebuked the unclean spirit, saying to it, 'Deaf and dumb spirit, I command you, come out of him and enter him no more!' Then the spirit cried out, convulsed him greatly, and came out of him. And he became as one dead, so that many said, 'He is dead.' But Jesus took him by the hand and lifted him up, and he arose." First of all, Jesus cast out the demon with a word of command. Then through His hands, He ministered healing power to the boy to strengthen him and raise him up.

5. *A Man with Dropsy* (see Luke 14:1-6). "He took him [by the hand] and healed him, and let him go."

6. *Malchus' Ear* (see Luke 22:49-51). "One of them [Peter] struck the servant of the high priest and cut off his right ear. ...And He [Jesus] touched his ear and healed him."

7. *Peter's Mother-in-law* (see Matthew 8:14-15; Mark 1:30-31; Luke 4:38-39). "Now when Jesus had come into Peter's house, He saw his wife's mother lying sick with a fever. So He touched her hand, and the fever left her. And she arose and served them."

8. *A Leper* (see Matthew 8:2-4; Mark 1:40-45; Luke 5:12-16). "Then Jesus put out His hand and touched him, saying, 'I am willing; be cleansed.' Immediately his leprosy was cleansed."

9. *Raising Jairus Daughter* (Matt 9:18-26; Mark 5:22-43; Luke 8:41-56). "Behold, a ruler came and worshiped Him, saying, 'My daughter has just died, but come and lay Your hand on her and she will live.' ...But when the crowd was put outside, He went in and took her by the hand, and the girl arose." This ruler had seen Jesus healing everyone through laying on of hands, and so requested Jesus to come and lay hands on her. He had no confidence that Jesus could heal her any other way. Jesus was happy to minister healing according to this method that Jairus had set.

The story of the healing of the centurion's servant (see Luke 7:1-10) started in a similar way, when Jesus was requested to come to the house to heal him, by touch. Again Jesus was content to follow this method if that was where the centurion's faith was. But when He got close to the house, the centurion expressed his faith that he believed Jesus could heal by the spoken word, of command alone, and that therefore the laying on of hands was not necessary. Jesus was pleased with his faith and his choice of a method of healing requiring a higher level of faith, and again He was happy to minister healing according to the method set by those receiving healing.

Jesus Heals

Thus we see that typically Jesus was happy to give healing power through whatever method the people chose. If they were ready to release their faith upon the laying on of hands or upon the spoken word, then Jesus would do that, because He wanted them healed.

In the healing of the nobleman's son (see John 4:46-54), Jesus was asked by the nobleman to come to his boy and heal him, by touch. As with most people, his faith was that he would be healed when Jesus laid His hands upon him; that was how the great majority of healings were done in His ministry.

However in this instance (perhaps because Jesus was not at liberty to make the journey and knowing his faith), Jesus called him to move onto a higher level of faith, and receive the healing through another higher method, the spoken word alone. The man believed the word, and his boy was healed. Therefore sometimes constraints of distance and time—there may be too many people needing prayer for there to be time to lay hands on all of them—require us to move onto a higher level of faith and use the spoken word alone, commanding healing power into their bodies.

This method does not have the same limits, for it can communicate the power over distance and to many people at the same time. Under normal circumstances, however, it is clear that the standard method Jesus used, which reflected His personal care for people, was the laying on of hands. Most people were ready to release their faith and receive their healing this way, whereas fewer were ready to operate on the higher level of believing the spoken word alone. I believe Jesus was happy for people to get healed either way!

10. *Two Blind Men at Capernaum* (see Matthew 9:27-34). "Then He *touched* their eyes, saying, 'According to your faith let it be to you.' And their eyes were opened."

11. *A Deaf Man* with a speech impediment (see Mark 7:32-37). "They brought to Him one who was deaf and had an impediment in his speech, and they begged Him to *put his hand* on him. He took him aside from the multitude, and put His *fingers* in his ears, and He spat and *touched* his tongue. Then, looking up to heaven, He sighed, and said to him, 'Ephphatha,' that is, 'Be opened.' Immediately his ears were opened, and the impediment of his tongue was loosed, and he spoke plainly."

12. *The Blind Man of Bethsaida* (see Mark 8:22-26). "He came to Bethsaida; and they brought a blind man to Him, and begged Him to *touch him*. So He took the blind man by the hand and led him out of the town. And when He had spit on his eyes and put his hands on him, He asked him if he saw anything. And he looked up and said, 'I see men like trees, walking.' Then He *put his hands on his eyes* again and made him look up. And he was restored and saw everyone clearly."

13. *Blind Bartimaeus* and one other Blind man at Jericho (Matthew 20:29-34; Mark 10:46-52; Luke 18:35-43). "Jesus had compassion and *touched* their eyes. And immediately their eyes received sight, and they followed Him."

In the healing services of Jesus, we also see His use of the laying on of hands. A healing service in Capernaum is described in Matthew 8:16 and

Mark 1:32-34 where many people were healed from all kinds of diseases. However, we have to turn to the account in Luke to find out what method was used: "When the sun was setting, all those who had any that were sick with various diseases brought them to Him; and He *laid His hands on every one of them and healed* them" (Luke 4:40).

Notice the phrase He healed them, which is often used—see Matthew 4:23, 9:35, 10:7-8, 14:14; Mark 6:12-13; Luke 6:19, 8:1-2, 9:2,6,11, 10:9; John 6:2. This indicates Jesus did not ask God to heal the sick, but instead He healed them directly by giving them the healing power that God had given Him at His anointing. He usually gave this healing power to the sick through the laying on of hands, as in this case. Thus He healed the sick by laying His Hands on them, imparting (administering) His healing power to their bodies.

He ministered in His hometown, Nazareth, but was unable to do any mighty work there, because of their unbelief:

> ...*He began to teach in the synagogue. And many hearing Him were astonished, saying, "Where did this Man get these things? And what wisdom is this which is given to Him, that such **mighty works** [healings] are **performed** by His hands!* (Mark 6:2)

From their response, it is clear that Jesus had taught them about healing through the laying on of hands, including testimonies of healings that had happened elsewhere by His hands.

> *Now He could **do** no mighty **work** there, except that He **laid His hands** on a few sick people and [in this way He] **healed** them. And He marveled because of their unbelief...* (Mark 6:5-6).

> *Now He did not **do** many mighty **works** [literally: works of power] there because of their unbelief* (Matthew 13:58).

Notice again that He was the one *doing* the *works of healing*, He was the One who healed the sick by means of the power of the Spirit or anointing upon Him. He wanted to do many works of power there, by ministering to them the healing power that was upon Him, but their inability to receive this power limited what He could do. They did not believe He was anointed, and so they could not receive His anointing.

However, even under these difficult conditions, He was able to heal a handful of sickly people through His hands. Even in this atmosphere of unbelief, a few people with minor ailments believed they could be healed through His hands. This shows us that the laying on of hands works when nothing else will, because people find it the easiest method to accept and use to release their faith. This is one reason Jesus used *touch* and the laying on of *hands* more than any other method to transmit healing to the sick.

One example of how God works through the laying on of hands is from my assistant Peter Hockley and his cousin. They had heard of a young woman who was in the hospital after having been in a serious car accident. The prognosis wasn't good. The next day they went to the Intensive Care Unit where she was in a coma and her parents told them that the doctors said if she ever did wake up she would have lasting brain damage and physical disability. The parents gave them permission to pray for their daughter. As they entered the room, it was a shock; she laid there motionless, as white as a ghost, with tubes and wires connecting her to machines that were keeping her alive. From her forehead and back across her scalp was a long, bloody incision that was stapled closed, the result of one of her surgeries.

Peter felt a flash of panic, but it was immediately replaced by something else rising up powerfully in him. He just knew God was going to heal her. They *laid* their *hands* on her and prayed, "Father God, we ask You to move right now and heal her. Raise her up from this bed, in Jesus' name." He commanded satan to take his hands off her and amazingly she began to shake in the bed at that very moment, before becoming still again. They only prayed for a few minutes and when they finished, she looked exactly the same, but they both felt a deep peace that God had worked a miracle.

After three days, they visited the hospital again, along with Pastor Hilary. The family was ecstatic when they saw them, saying that she had woken up from her coma without any trace of brain damage! The doctors were pleased, but completely astonished by the dramatic recovery. She was sleeping, though she looked totally transformed: her cheeks were flushed with color and the mark on her scalp was just a faint pink scar. They prayed a second time and

Hilary anointed her forehead with oil. Ten days later they returned to find out that she had made a full recovery and had gone home with her family. Jesus still heals today through the laying on of hands!

ANOINTING WITH OIL

The anointing with oil with the prayer of faith are variations of the laying on of hands, which uses the extra symbolism of *oil*. Laying on of hands is necessarily involved in the anointing with oil, but now in addition oil is applied as a *symbol* of the *healing anointing* of the Holy Spirit. It provides a perfect picture of what is happening spiritually when hands are laid on the sick one. Thus the oil is an outward sign of an inward grace, given as an aid to faith for the person receiving healing. It is a tangible reminder to them that when hands are laid upon them, the invisible healing anointing of God is flowing into them. When they have hands laid upon them and feel the oil, they are to know that God's anointing is upon them, and they are to believe they receive it.

We read about this in James 5:14-16:

> *Is anyone among you **sick**? Let him call for the elders of the Church, and let them **pray** over him, **anointing** him with oil in the name of the Lord. And the **prayer of faith** will **save** [heal] the sick, and the [power of the] Lord will raise him up. And if he has committed sins, he will be forgiven.*

There are five points to discuss regarding this Scripture passage and what people need to do if there are any among us who are sick:

I. They are to instruct the sick man in repentance and faith, to prepare him to receive his healing. He needs to be taught to receive forgiveness, through confessing any sins that might block his healing. He also needs to be taught to pray the prayer of faith, to believe he receives his healing, when he is anointed with the oil. It is the sick person that needs to believe he receives the healing power ministered to him.

2. They are to pray, coming into the presence of the Lord, thanking Him for His healing anointing freely given to the sick. And when they lay hands upon him and anoint him with oil, then His anointing will flow into the sick man and heal him.

3. They are to lay hands on him in the name of Jesus, anointing him with oil, believing that when they apply the anointing oil to him, then the healing anointing is also being applied to his body.

4. When the sick man is anointed, he is to receive this healing anointing through the prayer of faith, believing he receives it.

5. Then the Lord, by means of His healing power, will heal, save, the sick man of his sicknesses and raise him up into new life.

Notice also that two ingredients must be present for there to be success:

1. The power of the Lord.

2. The (prayer of) faith of the person.

God's power working through the man's faith does two things:

1. It saves him from his sickness, it drives out all disease.

2. It imparts new life and health to him, causing him to rise up.

FAITH IS NEEDED

But God's power, without the prayer of faith, will not work; our faith is needed to receive and give action to the power of God. This is emphasized by the phrase: "the prayer of faith will save the sick" (James 5:15). Now we know that it is the healing anointing of the Lord, represented by the oil, that actually heals the sick and raises him up. But since God's healing power will always flow when a sick person is anointed according to James 5, whether or not he is healed depends on whether he prays the prayer of faith and believes he receives it. Therefore it is essential that the sick person receives the power by faith.

It was Jesus Himself who instituted the anointing with oil, since we know the twelve disciples practiced it when they were sent out, "They departed and went through the towns *preaching* the Gospel and *healing* everywhere" (Luke 9:6). Mark gives us more detail:

> *They went out and **preached** that people should repent. And they cast out many demons, and **anointed with oil** many who were **sick**, and* [they] ***healed** them* (Mark 6:12-13).

Notice that they preached the Gospel first, then they healed the sick by the laying on of hands and anointing with oil. Jesus practiced this Himself and instructed His disciples to do it as well, when He sent them out. The fact that it says they "healed them" when they anointed them, confirms that the anointing with oil is done in connection with the method of ministering the healing anointing through the laying on of hands to the sick, who then receive it by faith. Thus although God is the Healer, the disciples are the venues of the healing, so it is true to say they healed them. But if it is true that James 5 is talking about receiving healing through prayer, when it is the elders who pray the prayer of faith for the sick, as is commonly believed, then to say that they healed them would be wrong, for it would be God, and God alone, who healed them.

Contact the Author

You can contact Derek Walker by email at d.r.walker@talk21.com.

If you have any questions from reading *Getting Healed*, or if you want more information about his other teaching materials, you can also go to his Website: www.oxfordbiblechurch.co.uk.

Additional copies of this book and other book titles from DESTINY IMAGE™ EUROPE are available at your local bookstore.

We are adding new titles every month!

To view our complete catalog online, visit us at:
www.eurodestinyimage.com

Send a request for a catalog to:

Via della Scafa, 29/14
65013 Città Sant'Angelo (Pe), ITALY
Tel. +39 085 4716623 • +39 085 8670146
info@eurodestinyimage.com

"Changing the world, one book at a time."

Are you an author?

Do you have a "today" God-given message?

CONTACT US

We will be happy to review your manuscript for the possibility of publication:

publisher@eurodestinyimage.com
http://www.eurodestinyimage.com/pages/AuthorsAppForm.htm